T0082805

MILLIONAIRE MIND-SET

What it Takes to Become a
Self Made Millionaire
A Step by Step Process
to Becoming Wealthy

KONATO WILLIAMS

MILLIONAIRE MIND-SET
WHAT IT TAKES TO BECOME A SELF MADE MILLIONAIRE
A STEP BY STEP PROCESS TO BECOMING WEALTHY

iUniverse books may be ordered through booksellers or by contacting:

iUniverse
1663 Liberty Drive
Bloomington, IN 47403
www.iuniverse.com
844-349-9409

Because of the dynamic nature of the Internet, any web addresses or links contained in this book may have changed since publication and may no longer be valid. The views expressed in this work are solely those of the author and do not necessarily reflect the views of the publisher, and the publisher hereby disclaims any responsibility for them.

Any people depicted in stock imagery provided by Getty Images are models, and such images are being used for illustrative purposes only.
Certain stock imagery © Getty Images.

Scripture taken from the King James Version of the Bible.

ISBN: 978-1-6632-1612-0 (sc)
ISBN: 978-1-6632-1613-7 (e)

Library of Congress Control Number: 2021900363

Print information available on the last page.

iUniverse rev. date: 01/28/2021

I dedicate this book to my father, who taught me at the age of eight to never take no for an answer. And to my children, with whom I share that same principle.

CONTENTS

INTRODUCTION

So many people look at the lives of rich, successful people and think about how wonderful their lives must be. How they would love to have rich people's lives, or their money to be more exact. As a frequent passing thought, we muse that these people must have exceptional talents that have put them in a class by themselves. Because these thoughts are rarely explored beyond this point by most people, success and riches remain just outside of their reach, simply to be admired by those who've made it.

We will find, however, that upon deeper inspection, the success achieved by those whom we admire came about as a result of doing something that each one of us can also do. More importantly, for most successful people, this success started with a similar thought where they admired someone who made it. The difference was simply the action taken after the thought.

For first-generation self-made millionaires, having wealth and being successful is primarily the result of hard work and positive thinking, coupled with networking with others and remaining focused on a goal. This process is available to all those who allow themselves to develop their dreams into visions, ideas, plans, and goals to achieve success. Money can and will surely come to you if you develop yourself accordingly, but your objective to sustain wealth must be rooted in a deeper passion than to simply possess a lot of money.

Money itself is a tool that is available to achieve your end result. It should not be your overall goal as an achiever to simply make money. There is a principle found in the attainment of it that should put the acquirer in a different mindset.

This book is designed to explore the self-made millionaire mindset and evaluate the causes that helped make them millionaires. What does it take to become a millionaire, and how does one maintain that status? Many life lessons can be learned from understanding this mindset, and these lessons can be useful to those who may not have achieved significant wealth but seek to structure their lives and improve the quality of their family dynamic to achieve this end.

The pursuit of wealth creates a mindset that embodies the spirit of our founding fathers and the early pioneers who helped to build and shape America. The lives of these honorable men and women still affect us today, and it would do all of us a great deal of good to study these individuals' minds. What were their visions? What motivated them to sacrifice themselves for the greater good of the whole? Many of them are found on our currency, but many are not. We can find among these great men a common bond that has indeed brought us right up to this point. We can find the core of the thinking of our founding fathers in the Declaration of Independence.

This document holds the very principles that are at the root of both business and politics. "We hold these truths to be self-evident, that all men are created equal, that they are endowed by their creator with certain unalienable rights. That among these are Life, Liberty, and the Pursuit of Happiness. That to secure these rights, governments are instituted among men, deriving their just powers from the consent of the governed."

This declaration paved the way for free trade and commerce inside America, thereby giving rise to a class of people who either migrated to America or grew up with the mindset to provide some form of service generating a continuous flow of money. Men like John D. Rockefeller Sr., Henry Ford, Andrew Carnegie, and many others are mentioned throughout this book not only to illustrate the evolution of many and the advancement of the country but also to detail a continuity of thinking from then to now. The same mindset that was present in those great men is still prevalent now among a great deal of millionaires and billionaires on a large scale.

On a smaller scale, there were countless others who provided various forms of service to the country and the world that helped advance society, making the lives of its inhabitants more convenient. To all those who have made a contribution to the betterment of humankind, we can never thank them enough. Our only means of showing our appreciation is to continue the work of service to our fellow man that so many have done before us. Leaving a legacy and sometimes a fortune that has helped to improve the lives of so many.

We will find at the root of the mind of most self-made millionaires a willingness to provide a service to their fellow man, who in return for this service show their appreciation by giving money.

We will find among this mindset a consistent pattern that can be followed by all those who work to develop themselves and adopt the attitude of service. This is a journey that will engulf your entire life. To that end, preparation is paramount. You will find in the pages of this book the "secret" keys for this preparation.

It is suggested that you put these principles to use in helping to discover your niches, finding what you're good at and love to do. It will become a wonderful process once you discover where you fit. Good luck.

Best wishes for your continued success,
Konato Williams

ACKNOWLEDGMENTS

To all those who have worked to advance America by providing some form of service, giving great examples of drive, determination, dedication, and the entrepreneurial spirit. I thank you for your work and your examples. Because of you all, America is able to enjoy a life of comfort and beauty, ranking among the world's superpowers.

God Bless America.

CHAPTER 1

Vision

Where there is no vision, the People Perish.
—Proverbs 29:18

Most people in life who have gained wealth and sustained it over a significant period of time envisioned themselves being successful long before success actually came. Going all the way back to childhood, vision is one of the most important qualities necessary to becoming successful. By looking into the lives of some of the most prominent people in America, in most of the men who helped to build and further the country, we will find a common trait.

Whether it came from an overbearing parent who envisioned a better future for his or her children or the children themselves being inspired by something within, at the root is a vision. School has, for the most part, two primary responsibilities: to educate the child academically, and to nurture the vision to discover how the child sees him- or herself and his or her relationship to the world.

We ask our children frequently throughout their childhood what or who they want to be when they grow up. From these questions, we tend to get a general understanding about what and who has inspired them. To this end, it is necessary that we start early to nurture success and that they develop focus. Those who have gained wealth and success are already aware of this fact, and they start by putting their children in the proper schools and social clubs, thereby creating a class of children where success will be bred into them through their environment and the influences they are around. Boarding and military schools are put in place to influence and direct the vision.

Vision is defined as "a mental picture, an image or concept in their imagination." Further explanation reads, "Far-sightedness, the ability to anticipate possible future events and developments."[1] As children, we are unaware of limitations. Nothing is impossible to children. You ask them what they want to be when they grow up, and many of them will quickly brighten up and tell you elaborate dreams and visions. Only through time, disappointments, and the realization of limitations are children brought back to a harsh reality. But in the back of their minds is a drive to achieve the impossible, to do the unlikely.

When we encourage our children to reach for the stars and tell them that nothing is impossible, we allow them the freedom to dream, to envision and create. The most creative people are those who do not believe in the impossible, who have encountered the right type of encouragement and were told the most important things that they can be told in their young lives.

"You can do anything you want to do!"

When we give our children the world, they create the reality that they want. As parents, we must remain rooted in reality, but we must let our children create their own worlds, for the future truly belongs to them. I am not encouraging allowing your child to remain in a fantasy world; give them powerful examples, and they will eventually learn to pattern themselves after them. Some of the most creative people who lived were viewed as "different."

A good example is Albert Einstein. He was looked at as weird, but his mind was not wired the same as most. At a young age, he came to the realization that he was different. From this belief, he was driven to discover different things. Because his mind was allowed to wonder, he developed the theory of relativity and revolutionized the world. This started with a vision with which many in the mainstream disagreed. Just because our children may seem different, we must watch them closely, learn to understand their personality, and make available to them everything that is necessary to nurture their vision.

Many of the most successful people in America, especially in politics and education, expect their children to follow in their footsteps; many families of doctors and lawyers started with very domineering parents, who had a vision of success for their children and believed that the path that they have charted is the best one for them. From a material standpoint, that may be true; this may or may not be the area where your child is most talented. Success in America is rather cookie-cutter style: follow the same steps others have followed and expect the same results. However, talent and mental development is the key to success as well, especially with the constant evolution of technology.

In order to understand the mindset of a millionaire, we must know about the good and the bad. The idea of the American dream is truly noble; to find and pursue your true chosen field is the actual result and manifestation of vision.

What do you hold dear in your heart that moves you? What thoughts wake you up in the mornings? I do not mean the dreading emotions that one may feel at a particular point in your life; these will pass as your conditions change. I am referring, however, to the thoughts, dreams, and desires that are at the core of your being. What wakes you up? What keeps you looking forward to your tomorrow? These are the thoughts that must be developed and nurtured. When we learn how to continuously identify our desires, these are the visions that reside at the core of our being.

Let us look at some of the men who helped develop America into one of the richest and most powerful countries in the world. In the late 1800s, Andrew Carnegie became one of the richest men in America. He was born in Scotland and came to America with his parents at a very young age. He started out investing in iron companies, eventually bought one in Pittsburgh, and went on to provide the steel that built many of the skyscrapers and other structures that still remain today. He retired in 1901 after selling his business to J. P. Morgan for $480 million, becoming one of the richest men in the world at that time. Much has been said about the tactics that he used to become successful. None of that is relevant. He made his mark on history and built over 2,500 libraries around the world to further the education of people. It has been said that he was not big on charity, but he gave away over $365 million throughout his life to advance America and the world. Clearly he felt that education was important.[2]

He also wrote several books after his retirement: *The Empire of Business*, *Problems of Today*, and his autobiography. He envisioned until his dying day a better America, and he used his tremendous resources to bring this about. From early on, he saw potential in his mind and dedicated himself to materializing the things of which he had a mental picture. The clarity of your vision will determine the strength and dedication to which you will work to manifest the things that are present in your mind.

Dale Carnegie (no relation to Andrew) was also quite busy. Sometime after Andrew Carnegie, he advanced principles designed to improve human relationships. Dale Carnegie wrote the widely acclaimed book *How to Win Friends and Influence People* in the 1930s, selling over fifteen million copies. He has been credited with one of the most popular phrases of that time, which can and will be useful for all time. He stated, "Believe that you can succeed and you will."[3] Undoubtedly, success must start with the belief that we can be successful. Another popular saying that deserves much acclaim is the popular slogan "Act as if." To act as if, we have in some way reached a desired place to ensure its realization because we have already in fact welcomed its coming. To act as if you are a millionaire can be disastrous, or it can become a self-fulfilling prophesy. To accept the fact that you want to become a millionaire in and of itself means nothing. Many people have dreams of becoming something that they cannot and will never realize. It is not because they cannot in all cases, but the dreams have to be based in something tangible. I cannot say that your dreams, whatever they are, cannot be realized. I say that your dreams must be attendant with hard work (action).

That being said, a dream of being a movie star and a vision of becoming a millionaire are based on two perspective realities. To become a millionaire means that first, you have to find your talent. Second, figure out how your talent or skill can serve others. Third, learn to professionalize your skill and make it marketable. You can search the earth and find millions of people who have become successful by making themselves useful to others.

How strong is your vision? How do you learn to identify your purpose in life? And how do you become useful to humanity? The key is learning how to serve others. As we get older, life starts to overwhelm us with the daily responsibilities of living. Thus, we rarely have the time to fully discover our natural talents and gifts. To this end, it is absolutely necessary that you take time to listen closely to that voice inside your head' some call it the alter ego or superego. This voice does the job of awakening us to greater being: a better person within ourselves. How often do we limit ourselves by not adhering to this voice, failing to hear the higher calling beckoning us onward to our true purpose in life?

We quickly act to silence this voice because of the cares of this world and our daily responsibilities. But it will not be silenced because it is calling us from our innermost longing to achieve something great with our lives. Most people know that they're born to do something great with their lives, but they cannot rightfully state what that is. I would argue that the reasons for this is partly because people have not listened to the voice within themselves.

Nevertheless, there is a driving force that keeps pushing us, telling us that we should be doing something greater. Take for example Fran Lubbs, who after climbing the corporate ladder did not find happiness and wanted to return to her first love of running a child nursery. She says, "The higher you move up the corporate ladder and the larger the corporation becomes, you lose touch with what happens in the business everyday. I wanted to get back in the schools. I missed the kids—They're a constant reminder of what's good and beautiful in the world." After making it high up in the corporate world, she listened to a deeper calling and, after many years, left the corporate world and became a part of a nursery school franchise. Regardless of age, it is never too late to find your purpose in life and to start listening closely to the voice. Learn to tap into the greatest intelligence that is present in your mind and discover your gift. Scientists have said that most people use only one-tenth of their brain capacity, meaning that most of us go about our daily lives like robots, feeding the most basic urges that we have: food, sex, and comfort. Once these urges are met, we're satisfied. Rarely do we tap into the genius that wants action and stimulation. We simply deaden this with some form of basic entertainment.

Not so with the successful among us. They utilize more of their brain power and find out the desires of the people who have no interest in advancing beyond basic needs. As an aspiring millionaire, you must learn to constantly develop your mental awareness. Key to this is discovering your purpose in life. One billionaire, Leon Black, founder of Apollo Global Management, advises, "Start your career in a place where there is a lot of action. A lot of smart people who understand risk and reward and action. Learn to be patient and learn to be opportunistic."[5]

It has been said that our actions spring out of what we fundamentally desire with our lives. This can be on a primitive level, or it can help us to reach our highest heights. Once we can see past our primitive urges for the basic essentials in life—food, clothing, shelter, love, and sex—we can then learn to focus the lens on our lives and envision greater days. To begin to visualize, plan and then execute your plan. That is the foundation necessary to build a successful life.

Henry Ford was one of the greatest Americans who ever lived. Because of him, America has grown due to the ability to travel great distances by automobile. Ford became interested in automobiles as a young man. He established Ford Motor Company and revolutionized the automobile industry with the assembly line method, allowing Ford to produce and sell more cars at a lower price. From 1908 to 1927, more than half the cars in the United States were Fords. Ford passed the savings he made from his assembly line production to his customers, making his cars affordable to the average American family.[6]

Ford Motor Company has gone through many adjustment periods, but it still remains one of the big three American auto makers today, providing transportation and employment to millions of people. The market at the time of Henry Ford was wide open, allowing him to capitalize on it. The point is that he envisioned a company that could provide a service to advance the country. By listening to the voice within himself and not being deterred by his detractors, he pioneered the auto industry. Today, Ford Motor Company functions as a corporation with an executive board of directors. The corporate office acts as the brains of the company and finances people to develop new concepts and ideas for cars that will continue to meet the demands of the future. Thus, they pay people to visualize ideas that may become tomorrow's new cars and trucks. These people must carefully study the needs and wants of the people, and then they go in labs and develop concepts based on the needs they have discovered. From these studies, marketing strategies were established to catch the attention of the masses. Studying the function of the most successful corporations can provide wonderful examples of how the millionaire mindset operates in a group. Vision is paramount, but without the proper action, it is naught but a dream.

Joseph Patrick Kennedy was a man of vision who put his vision into action, looking far in the future he, with his wife, set out to make his mark on history. At the age of twenty-five, he gained control of a small bank in East Boston, becoming the youngest bank president in the United States. He invested his money in stock, bonds, and real estate, among other things, making himself a millionaire. Having high expectations for the future, he groomed his four sons for power and success, ensuring that they received the proper education. As he grew in wealth, his influence also grew with his family.

His sons, Joseph Jr., John Fitzgerald, Robert, and Edward were a tightly knit group of brothers who believed in the success of the family. Following the leadership of their father, they adhered to a systematic method of advancement where the eldest brother, Joseph, was to take the family into politics with the remainder being in full support, waiting for instruction and guidance from their father. However, there was the untimely death of Joseph Jr. while in service to his country: he died on a risky mission when his military plane, full of hazardous material, exploded. Saddened by the death of his oldest son, Joseph Sr. continued to guide his sons to fulfill his plans for the family. Thus, John entered politics. Upon entering, he shared these words about the planned ascent of his family: "Just as I went into politics because Joe died, if anything happens to me tomorrow, my brother Bobby would run for my seat in the Senate. And if Bobby died, Teddy would take over for him."[7] Wow, here was a well-thought-out plan expressed by a man who, ten years later, would become the youngest elected president of the United States. Clearly, these plans had originated long before John F. Kennedy decided to enter politics. He was followed by both his brothers Robert and Edward. The Kennedy dynasty is a wonderful example of a father with a vision galvanizing his children to fulfill that vision. Because of his vision, his family will always be a part of American history.

In technology, there was a young high school boy and his friend who saw the potential in computers that would advance his country. Bill Gates set up his first company with his schoolmate Paul Allen, when Bill was only fifteen years of age. These young boys developed a software system that was used at the time of IBM, who initially had no idea that two high school boys developed the new software system. Nevertheless, their talent could not be ignored. IBM went on to use their system. However, Bill Gates and Paul Allen had bigger dreams, and they put them into action, developing Microsoft and becoming the largest computer company in the world.[8] Bill Gates and Paul Allen went on to become two of the richest men in the world.

President John F. Kennedy, during his inauguration said, "Ask not what your country can do for you. Ask what you can do for your country."[9] To deliberate what you can do for your country is a question that can lead you toward your life's work and untold riches. The people mentioned in this book are highlighted because of their contribution to humankind. From this service, most of them grew mentally, spiritually, and financially and had a healthy respect for humankind. The most important thing to do is think and visualize.

To do this, brief periods of isolation may be necessary. This isolation is very important because it allows us time for introspection. We can't achieve anything without first getting a grip on our mental processes and the emotional responses that become second nature to most of us. In order to chart a course for yourself, you must be in tune with who you are. Discover what you want out of life and learn your true potential.

We are capable of so much more if we first learn to discover who we are. I personally could not achieve anything substantive until I answered this question. There are so many images in the world that we identify with, that we can lose ourselves in, and we may never know who we are. To understand who you are, you need time to analyze yourself. What do you absolutely love to do that is beneficial to others and that you're also good at? Discover some of the things you enjoy doing, and you can find part of your true personality. As Queen Latifah said, "I feel beautiful when I'm doing what I love."[10]

Once you can identify the person who you are, you have found the first key. We must learn to dig further into our character. Our parents, siblings, and close friends, who have known us for many years and watched us grow, can help with this endeavor. Once you discover more keys, then you must use them to unlock the door of your mind. I am certain that on the other side, you will find something that you can use to provide a service to humanity.

You must be ever mindful that how you think as you go about this process is equally as important, if not more so, as you partake on this journey. If you enter this process but your mind is not filled with a love for humanity and a desire to serve, then you will not find it. The basic ingredient to finding your purpose in life is to be of service in some way. Even if it is simply to offer positive encouragement to others, our thoughts are most important. Being filled with anger and hatred will not allow you to see the beauty in yourself or others. Start by first being in a positive state of mind.

Dale Carnegie expressed that the best attitude is necessary in order to grow into your own greatness. He advised, "Learn to love, respect and enjoy other people."[11] Learning to develop a love and respect for other people gives us the tools necessary to serve others and makes them more accepting of your service. There are many examples of people who are in the business of service, but do not have the attitude or disposition to serve. We shall not use any of them here because they do not deserve a place in history other than for us to learn from them how not to be.

We must learn to enjoy other people. Bear in mind that as you begin to build your future of service to humanity, the key to finding yourself and identifying your relationship to others, as well as finding your place in the world, has a lot to do with how you relate to other people.

There will always be someone to help you, whether it be by words of guidance or other means that will assist you in realizing your purpose. However, these people certainly will not do so if your attitude is negative.

Warren Thompson, CEO of Thompson Hospitality Corp, heads a company that owns twenty-one retail franchises and manages 550 contract locations in schools, hospitals, and corporate dining centers. Thompson projected generating revenues of $390 million for 2011. He has grasped one of the most important keys to handling people and customer service. He said, "We try to hire attitude. We can teach skills and develop skills, but the person has to have the right attitude. We have to have people in our business who smile by nature."[12]

So important is your attitude to your success that with every step you take toward your goals, you must constantly be aware of your feelings about what you're doing and whom you're doing it with. G. Jean Davis, CEO of Unibar Services Inc., helps us to focus this idea while offering these words: "If you surround yourself with good people and provide a clear vision of where you want to go and what's in it for them, you can be successful."[13]

To surround yourself with good people, you have to be able to recognize the good qualities in others. Before you can find these qualities in others, you must first find them in yourself and nurture them. Learning to be a good person will help you find the good in others. Nurturing your own good qualities will introduce you to the best in yourself. From this, you can envision a brighter future where you're able to serve humanity. Take the time to search your soul for the good in you. It will amaze you. There is an interconnectedness that binds us to each other, and once we bring this out, it will attract others to you.

There is a medical terminology called autogenetic conditioning. Its definition is simple: self-producing or self-produced. It is vitally necessary to begin conditioning yourself for success by constantly telling yourself that you will be successful. Create the world you want for yourself by visualizing it and then accepting it. From this we will produce it because we have conditioned ourselves to produce it.

"Believe you can succeed, and you will."

CHAPTER 2

Leadership

Leadership is defined as "the ability to lead—the ability to guide direct or influence people."[1] Having leadership is one of the most important qualities necessary in order to become successful in any field of business. What are some of the primary qualities of a leader, and how do you know whether you possess them? Human nature has equipped each of us with as innate ability to lead and follow. This is most noticeable in early childhood, when we are capable of expressing primitive urges. Children as early as one year old seek to take some degree of control over their little lives. They no longer want to be fed; they want to feed themselves. They want to put on their own clothes and take some control. They cannot explain why this need is there, only that it is a desire they possess to have some control over what happens to them.

As we get older, our minds are like sponges, soaking up and processing all of the information around us. In fact, during these early years, the child's brain is most active, processing information and people. The primary reason for this process is reception and perception. The child is first receiving information and then learning how to perceive it, be it in either a positive or negative light. Only two basic emotions are felt by the child: like or dislike.

It learns to mimic the people close to it, taking both their good and bad characteristics and growing from them. Children display the most important aspect of leadership for us to learn from: the ability to follow. Every successful leader started as a good follower, whether of a trend, a particular field, or a person. Being able to tune into another person is uppermost in being successful. To understand the needs and wants of people, we must have a general understanding of human nature and people's needs to follow that which is successful.

Bernard B. Beal, CEO of M. R. Beal and Co., a money management investment company worth over $1.6 billion, had this to say about people's need for leadership. "I really wanted a business plan where everybody just worked, knew what to do, and did it, and there was no hierarchy, I just didn't want the hierarchical structure. But as human beings we are herd animals who require a leader. If there isn't a leader, then the herd stampedes or scatters."[2] Without the critical element inside of us as humans to follow, we could not gain information necessary to develop and survive.

Bill Gates, clearly one of the most successful people of this era and the richest man in the world for many years, provided good insight in his book *The Road Ahead*. "I'm not an educator, but I'm a learner, and one of the things I like about my job is that I'm surrounded by other people who love to learn."[3]

While in the learning stages, we discover the tools necessary to be successful leaders. Through learning, we find the patterns in human behavior that we must understand in order to provide a service. Henry Ford's words of wisdom provides us with much guidance with respect to this discovery: "If there is any one secret of success it lies in the ability to get the other person's point of view, and seeing things from that person's angle as well as from your own."[4] In our study of leadership, we quickly find a pattern of behavior among both the people and the leaders, so although learning about the people is tantamount to leading, your mindset while gaining this information is equally important.

Burrell Communications Group LLC, with revenues worth $21 million, described the steps taken to launch a successful company. These words are offered on how they have built a prominent advertising agency: "A company's success and influence are defined by its leaders ability to identify a need, capture an audience and adapt to environmental change to maintain a dominant market position."[5]

Being receptive to different types of personalities helps develop you into a well-rounded person and helps gain an understanding into the various patterns of human behavior. To obtain wealth means that you must find a need in society and then fill it. This is a journey that usually takes time because the education process must be advanced enough to identify the needs of each group of people that you seek to serve. Patterns in human behavior can be broken down into a few simple principles. First, to understand the most important human need. After the essentials of, food, clothing, and shelter, it is emotional. Love and respect are at the top of every human being's sense of self-worth, and people's view of the world is based on this expression.

Take for example a child who has grown up without a constant expression of love from his or her parents but a constant demand for respect. While growing up, this child may be angry a lot and could easily become violent if it feels disrespected. Yet the craving at the root of its being is for love, because this is something it has been lacking since early childhood. It will often go through life unable to express love until a loving, patient individual teaches it. Once it learns how to love, it often loves more intensely and appreciate its beauty, because it now has something it has been lacking. This is a case to the extreme. Learning what motivates people will help you in your rise.

Many years ago, Dale Carnegie shared with us one of the most profound needs in human nature. He shared the words of one of America's profound philosophers of the 1930s, Dr. John Dewey: "The deepest urge in human nature is the desire to be important." This desire fills one of the great needs mentioned earlier: respect. Make people feel that they're respected, and they will be open to your suggestions and happily listen to your views, if they know that their own views are also valued and respected.

Bill Gates built one of the most successful corporation in the world. Microsoft produced components for computers that helped advance the world. He also helped create a cadre of millionaires through his company. In his own words, here is one of the ways he unified his company: "When I was preparing to take my company public. I arranged to distribute an unusually large share of ownership to employees. It was a way of letting them know how much their performance mattered."[6] Having a healthy respect for your employees or the people that you're trying to reach will lead you to success.

As important in our research is the motivation of love. Love is the most powerful human emotion. When you're able to identify what a person loves, you have discovered his thumbscrew, his weak spot, which can inspire great highs or extreme lows. The love a person has for himself and his family drives him to spend money. Having an appreciation for this can allow us to fulfill a need that has made many people very wealthy. Burrell Communications Group and CEO Fay Ferguson have sought to be at the forefront of their field, with a keen focus on marketing to their African American audience. Ferguson explains, "We always start from a strategic standpoint. That's very important to us. We truly try to understand the African American consumer, what motivates them, what's going to compel them to buy this product or service over a competitors. So we study the segment and we truly go about making sure that when we bring a plan to our clients that its data driven."[7]

This is a major part of the process necessary to understand and develop the mindset of a millionaire. To develop into a successful leader, you must adhere to the process. There is a difference between a manager and a leader. There are many successful managers who reside over many million- and even billion-dollar companies. It is advantageous to study these successful people. They are often well educated and skilled in the art of following. Along the way to becoming a successful leader, you may become a well-refined manager. However, some people have an innate ability to lead and never function as managers of other people's empires. They are driven by a force within themselves that makes them unique beings who are worthy of study. In looking into the lives of most millionaires, though, we will find that they followed the process and traveled through the proverbial ranks to become the examples that we now study.

Oprah Winfrey is another exceptional example of a person who traveled through the ranks. She came from a humble beginning and became the first African American female billionaire after having chosen a career in journalism. After moving with her father in Tennessee and attending Tennessee State University, she became the youngest person to anchor a newscast. While learning the business, she was being called to a greater service than to just provide news. She went on to become a nationally syndicated talk show host and established her own TV and film production studio, Harpo Productions. Oprah has, over the course of more than twenty years, impacted the lives of perhaps millions of people—and did I say she was a billionaire?

Her leadership style, as displayed publicly, seems to be relaxed but focused. Learning to develop an effective management or leadership style is very important. Generally, most leaders are type-A personalities and are more extroverted. This leadership style is partly based on how you perceive yourself and how you relate to others. In order to understand what it will take to be successful, you must maximize your potential. Self-actualization is important to this process. Your perception of yourself, others, and your environment will help develop your latent talents and abilities. This may not necessarily be taught in schools. It comes from individuals who are aware of your talents; that is, they see those talents shining through your personality, and they seek to bring them out of you through a process of self-realization. Shakespeare, one of the greatest writers of all time, makes a profound statement: "Assume a virtue, if you have it not." So powerful is that regarding helping us develop not only the dormant talents but also the talents for which we aspire. To see a virtue, a trait that we wish to obtain can be critical to becoming successful. Finding our strengths not only is a wonderful venture in terms of emotional happiness and peace; it can and will arm you with the necessary ammunition to launch a life of prosperity. Therefore, the first goal in growing into a well-refined person and active leader is the ability to identify your strengths and weaknesses in your personality and involvement with others.

Equally important is the ability to recognize the personality types of those with whom you associate. Your colleagues can play a very important role in your rise. If you do not identify the various wolves and sheep, you can be bogged down unnecessarily, wasting a lot of time with the wrong type of people, and you will not advance as quickly as you would if you avoided such people.

In 1956, Warren Buffett borrowed money from relatives and friends and formed an investment firm; he later paid back these loans thirty times over. Buffett went on to become one of the richest man in the world. Had he not had trusted friends and family to believe and invest in him, he may not have excelled the way he did. Because he had people who believed in him and backed him financially, he became a man whose words alone make other people money with Berkshire Hathaway. Conversely, there is a part of success that cannot be ignored, and every successful person has had to carry this burden at some point. Take the jealous colleague who believes that you should not be where you are. This person often comes up with you in your rise to power, but they have not received the same benefits you have. If you take over leadership of an existing company, this person may be the one who feels that they have been skipped over. How you deal with such people will be important to creating harmony within your company, and it will be a true test to your leadership and character.

Every company has people who may not completely pull their weight and may even be riding on the coattails of someone else's talent. These people can often be wolves in sheep's clothing and will seek to undermine you at every turn. Whether it is in trying to show how inept you are in your decision making or simply as backstabbers, these people are very poisonous to your progress, and they must be addressed at your earliest opportunity before their poison takes root.

Under most circumstances, the best way to deal with these types of people is through professionalism and kindness. In the work environment, you may not always have your whole team on board in your decision making. You must spare no effort in uniting your team behind you, but there will be times when you must make major decisions that may not be popular with some of your employees. You must be mindful of those who do not truly have the best interests of you or the company at heart. The moment you identify these types, you must remove them from the company. If firing them is not feasible, then you must isolate them and never give them important responsibilities.

Leadership has in itself many dynamics, and in finding the one that best fits your personality, you must find people who will fill in the voids that your style may not suit. One example is if you're more of an aggressive personality, you will need to have someone who is more relaxed in leadership style. If you have more of a hands-on approach, where you're the type to roll up your sleeves and work alongside your people, you will need someone very close to you who has more of a clerical style. Whatever your style, you must find people to complement your leadership style with one of their own.

It is all about the people and knowing how to make them respond to you. The best way to do this is through always being humble. An old Chinese sage said twenty-five centuries ago, "The reasons why rivers and seas receive the homage of a hundred mountain streams is that they keep below them. Thus, they are able to reign over all the mountain streams. So the sage, wishing to be above men, putteth himself below them; wishes to be before them he putteth himself behind them. Thus, though his place be above men they do not feel his weight; though his place be before them, they do not count it an injury."[8]

A strong management team is a must in order to acquire millions. Understanding the benefit of team meetings and how you unite the team around your idea is critical to reaching substantial heights. You have to get in front of the right people, and they will look at the strength of your team, their unity, and their attitude toward whatever it is you're trying to do. "It's hard to invest in something that is just an idea. Asking for funding for an idea so you can quit your job and develop it isn't entrepreneurship, it's moving from one job to another."[9]

If your goal is to build a multi-million-dollar company with very little start-up capitol, your business plan is critical, and how you attract investors to your plan can spell the difference between success and failure. To that end, a basic study in human nature will work wonders for you. In order to be a leader in industry, you must cater to the needs of the people. Thus, leadership style in business is likened to leading from the back, where you can see the movement ahead before you reach it. Studying the trends that can advance your company is your most important job. Leading from the rear does not mean taking a relaxed approach by any stretch of the imagination. You must educate yourself about the field into which you wish to go. You must first look at the market and its appeal to your audience.

Research is important to any venture. Your research should be geared toward learning the spending power of this group and their spending habits. As with fashion, the leaders are the designers; so too with business. The leaders are the entrepreneurs who take the time to develop research on their perspective markets. The advertising agency Burrell Communications Group, company CEO Fay Ferguson, and McGhee Williams-Osse have learned this very important principle in business. Williams-Osse explains that finding a target audience helps advance a company's brand, targeting a young audience called yurban, meaning urban youth, which she explains is "a group of young people between the ages of 18 and 30 who are connected in terms of mindset and life style, rather than ethnicity, geography, or demographics. It's more about mindset. Many millennials fall into this category. They represent more than $200 billion in spending power."[10]

To develop a product for a market with a spending power upward of $200 billion is certainly worth taking the time to research different strategies to capture this market. Here is a good example of why leadership is so vitally important, as well as why the most successful people have hired the greatest minds to figure out the spending power and marketability of each audience. This audience may have a spending power of $200 billion, but there are various others to be explored with totally different tastes. Your ability to reach them will depend on your team and its ability to connect with them. Rest assured that if you do not have the money to hire the elite marketing team, you can still play with the big boys and be as successful if you simply learn the rules to the game and play them. It may seem that many of the players are ruthless and have no real principles, but there is indeed a code of ethics by which most millionaires live. Those in the entertainment industry may not necessarily observe the same rules of engagement that most entrepreneurs live by, but they become the exception, not the norm. In fact, roughly 2 percent of the rich and superrich are entertainers. Thus, their lifestyles may consist mainly in excessive spending of money such as paying $2 million for a pair of shoes or $250,000 for diamond-encrusted teeth. These examples are not indicative of the millionaire mindset or of good leadership to that end. Although these individuals may be rich, they do not appreciate the value of being wealthy.

It is indeed the right of millionaires to spend their money on whatsoever they choose, but this study is focused on a concentrated form of wealth, that is, core values of the wealthy and how they can be used to establish and maintain wealth. The mindset is the key, and we focus on leadership examples to gain models that can be used to acquire wealth. The general code among the wealthy is to provide service.

To illustrate my point, the United States of America has approximately five hundred billionaires, and 70 percent of them are self-made. What were some of the steps they took to get to that point? There is indeed a common thread that binds these billionaires together—a code, so to speak, that puts them in the 0.000001 percentile of the world. Their fields of work may be different, but most of them started with an idea geared toward providing a service or product to the world. They all had a team of professionals that were instrumental in building a company or group of companies that impacts the world. With a group of successful women at the home of Facebook, COO and self-made billionaire Sheryl Sandberg offers advice to the distinguished group of women professionals. Regarding one of her dinner guests, Cisco CEO John Chambers, Sandberg said, "What he understood is that it wasn't about having women in your company, but about having women in leadership roles … If you have the best talent, you're going to have the best performance."[11]

In your quest to become a self-made millionaire, it would be wise to study not only the trends that can bring wealth but also the patterns of behavior of the rich and successful. Start with your education, whether it be college, the school of hard knocks, your present company, or simply your vision to become wealthy. The process starts with finding successful patterns to study. Thus, at the root of your mentality must be a willingness to learn from others. These will be your most important lessons on your path to wealth and having control of your business, whether you're in a managerial role or your own boss. Being aware and in tune with others will help you become successful.

The code of ethics that should be adopted by a leader in business is as follows

* Always observe the Golden Rule: treat others the way you want to be treated.

* Surround yourself with smart people who want to see you succeed and who are a part of the mission both at heart and in mind. Having different people around you is a cardinal rule that should always be observed. Always look to promote the people who show intelligence, drive, and dedication to the company. Avoid sycophants and yes-men because they disguise their true intentions. They are usually power hungry and out for themselves. A large part of your leadership may be spent sifting these types from your midst.

* Always be the example of good leadership. You should be the early riser. Be the first at your company getting the day started. On occasion, you should have coffee ready when your employees arrive to work. To expect the best from others, you must show them the best of yourself. To become this, you must always put your best foot forward and greet your employees with a smile and an open heart.

* Expect the best from your employees. Give them a standard to live up to, and they will have a goal on which to focus their energy.

Charles Schwab once had a factory whose production was below expectations. To stimulate the groups, who had two shifts, he asked one of the crew leaders their number of production for that day. Once informed of their number, he wrote it boldly on the floor, where the second shift could see it. Upon their arrival at work, they inquired about the number and its meaning. After being told that the big boss was in and wrote it regarding the production number of the previous shift, they promptly set out to beat the number, and at the end of the shift, they replaced the number with their own higher quota. This started a production that greatly increased the amount of products made by this plant.

* Work to unify your company, and employees will reach great heights. The key is your ability to connect with your employees, or having someone who can.

* Be available to your employees, Based on the size of your company, this may seem hard. However, the larger you become, the more important this will be. If you have businesses all over the world, you must take the time to periodically travel to all of them and interact with your employees. From your highest, most-valued employees to the ones cleaning your floors, learn to appreciate all of them, hear their concerns, and do all you can to make them happy. They are truly your bread and butter.

When all of your employees know that you care for and want the best for them, they will be happy and productive, knowing that they were able to address their concerns with the big boss, who listened to them attentively and not dismissively. That will help make more cooperative employees. Try to remember as many people's names as you can, especially of your employees.

* Have regular meetings with your management staff. It is very important that a leader has unity with the troops. Your company should function as one organization, where people know their roles and are skilled in their fields. You should know the strengths and weaknesses of your management team. A good leader knows how to use the

strengths of his team and help members make their weak points strong. You will find that different personalities clash at these meetings. This is where you will be able to grow as well. You may naturally find yourself inclined toward one view more than the other. At these times, you must remain neutral and seek to find the good points in each person's point of view. Having a group of managers will usually lead to some sort of conflict, because each will hold strong views. Again, remain neutral and allow yourself to hear both sides.

* Keep a positive attitude. The sun does not shine every day. You and your company will go through ups and downs. Every relationship goes through good and bad times. This is life. The strength of the relationship will be tested most during these difficult times. So too with any business. At the bad times, you have to weather the storm. Your business will be tested most during your downs. The key to coming out of these difficult times is to keep the right attitude. See through the dark times, and you will get through them!

These principles of leadership are important not only in business but also on an interpersonal level. How you handle people in your personal life can affect how you deal with professionals in business. On the road to becoming a millionaire, recognize the code of ethics and apply them in your pursuit of a successful business. Also use these ethics to improve the quality of your life. You will find a greater degree of difficulty succeeding in other areas of life if your attitude is not positive. Have a positive outlook on life.

Your frame of mind is everything.

CHAPTER 3

Motivation

Motivation is a character trait that is a stimulus-causing action. The energy level behind the stimuli can determine the magnitude of the result. It is a behavior that is rooted into the physiology and mental makeup of the human being. Behavioral scientists have identified two main aspects of motivational behavior.

> Arousal behavior, which means to be "stirred up ready for action." It could result from stimuli from inside or outside of the body. Further, "an aroused organism's response to stimuli depends on habits and other ways of acting that it has learned."

> Direction of behavior, which is determined by several influences such as organisms, skills, habits, general capacities, and motives, which can be a cause to direct behavior. The direction of behavior can be more related to external influences that can stimulate action.[1]

There are also types of motives that cause behavior, such as homeostatic motives, which include, hunger, thirst, respiration, and excretion; they work to keep the body in a balanced internal state. There are also nonhomeostatic motives, which include sex, nest building, and curiosity about the environment; these motives are aroused by occasional forces. Last is <u>learned</u> motives or social motives, which include curiosity, desire for novelty, and need for such things as achievement, power, social affiliation, and approval. Learned motives continue to endure and influence behavior throughout life.[1]

People in life are motivated at different times to do different things. The motivation to be rich and successful can be rooted in a number of environmental factors, from early childhood throughout life. It may act as an ongoing period of influence or a brief encounter. Whatever has caused the motivation, it is very important to keep it and evolve the motivation into a solid plan of action. Mayer Amschel Rothschild started as a banker in Frankfurt, Germany, at a time when Jews were being persecuted, causing them to keep their money circulating in their small community. Mr. Rothschild founded the banking dynasty by making profitable investments for the royal families of his day. He had five sons and trained them in money management. Upon his death, he refused to name a single heir to his substantial fortune. Instead, he instructed his sons to remain united and expand the family business. Following their father's wishes, the sons branched out all over Europe, spreading to five different countries and establishing banking institutions in each. They consolidated the banks into one, becoming "The House of Rothschild." Their influence is still felt today throughout the banking world.[2]

Mayer Amschel was motivated by a desire to escape the world of poverty and establish a name for his family; this desire started in his childhood. By going back into the childhood of many of the self-made millionaires, we will find many motivational factors that traveled with them into adulthood. In fact, we learn many of our patterns of behavior as children. Thus, by understanding drive and correcting it if necessary, we trace our behavior and our thinking back to our childhood. "As children develop, they copy some behavior of many models, including their friends as well as their parents. They combine aspects of behavior into patterns through direct and observational learning and cognitive growth. They also acquire standards and values that help them regulate and evaluate their own behaviors."[3]

T. Boone Pickens is a good example of having a motivational factor from childhood that carried him throughout his life, putting him in the billionaires club for quite some time. He is presently worth over $900 million. He says, "I've always loved making money, and since that first paper route, I've never been broke."[4] He can be viewed as an achiever with a motivational factor geared toward achievement and power.

To motivate is "to make somebody feel enthusiastic, interested, and committed to something: cause somebody's behavior; to be the cause or driving force behind something that somebody does." To be motivated is defined as "having enough interest or incentive to do something." To have motivation means "A feeling of interest or enthusiasm that makes somebody want to do something that causes such feeling. A reason for doing something or behavior in some way. PSYCHOL—forces determining behavior, the biological, emotional, cognitive, or social forces that activate and direct behavior."[5] Take the time to think about what it is that motivates you every day. Know that motivation can be a learned behavior, and therefore it is occasional. In other words, what motivated you yesterday may not be the same thing that motivates you today. Therefore, think about what it is you want to do. Are there any examples present that you can learn from?

Developing the mindset of a millionaire may require a complete paradigm shift. Your mindset may not necessarily need to be completely shifted in order for you to focus and tune in on the correct goals. To become a self-made millionaire, your energy must be set on it first. This may require time, because it is a deliberate process that you must work at. A complete makeover may be necessary, starting with the way you think. The first step in this process of becoming somebody important is to act like somebody important now. Thus, your drive should be to develop the necessary qualities. Please know that the examples to take should be from those who acquired their wealth the legal way. Although shrewdness is indeed important, unethical examples will not lead to long-term success.

Work on developing yourself, taking some of the good qualities that you find in those who have become successful. This part of the journey to make yourself into a millionaire should be your most enjoyable work. Mold yourself into the person you see yourself as, and you will attract people to help you facilitate your goals. Andrew Carnegie started his life in poverty working for two cents an hour. He died one of the richest men in the world in his day.

Preparation is the key to achieve this end. This may sound cliché, but it is true nonetheless that "proper preparation prevents poor performance." Being prepared for something before it happens can equip you to handle it whenever it comes. Thus, this study is designed to enlighten about the general mindset of millionaires and successful people in business, politics, and general living. To prepare is to start the process of being successful. It is said that God will not give you a gift until you have first prepared to receive it.

This preparation can come in many forms. Struggles, adversity, and hardship can be means of preparation. But this can also lead to excess once the burden is removed. However, it should usually lead to success and prosperity if the person has the right mindset. How do you prepare for wealth? During an interview, NFL Super Bowl–winning quarterback Drew Brees provides these words: "Obviously most guys in the NFL are type A personalities, that's how we got here in the first place. You need to have the drive and work ethic to get to this level, and a lot of that carries over to what we do off the field. You see lots of guys get involved in business. I think we're all used to being successful, we're used to being able to go out and accomplish a goal or task or whatever it might be."[6]

Understand that we attract to us that which we are. You may wonder why you have the type of spouse that you have, or why your life is the way that it is. Not only is our life as we grow older based on a series of decisions that we make, taking us from one circumstance to another, but tomorrow is solely based on what we do today. The type of friends that you have and everything that surrounds you is based on how you think—not so much the thoughts that you may have from moment to moment, but the core beliefs that motivate your actions both long and short term. These thoughts are indeed firmly rooted, but they are not permanent. Thus, we can chance our entire internal reference, but it is not an overnight process and requires concentration of thought.

You may ask why some things seem so easy to some while it comes so hard for you. If you pay close attention to that person's attitude and outlook on life, there is something in the person that seems to breathe success. Even when these people are not successful, their attitudes seem to emit confidence. For the most part, these individuals possess a winning attitude. Their outlook on life is to win no matter the odds, and they have convinced themselves that they are going to win.

This attitude seems to excite and motivate them. Those whom they encounter become infected with their spirit and attitude, and they believe in these people because they seem to know exactly what it is they want. And they're on the way to getting it. Those whom they come in contact with are happy to assist them in their pursuit. Look at it this way: Think of a child whom you have never met who comes to you asking for something. This child seems to speak as if not only are they sure of what they're talking about, but they are also convinced that they will achieve what they have in their mind. You do not sense the slightest hint of doubt from this child because they do not have it. Not only are they convinced that they will succeed, but they are equally convinced that you're going to help them. You would be hard pressed not to grant the wishes of this child for several reasons.

First, you want to encourage the confidence. Second, in your mind, you begin to believe that maybe this child will one day be somebody, and you want to help nurture them into that, so you push this aspirant to greater heights. Third, you simply admire the audacity of this child and want to see this ambitious youngster succeed. Now apply this to the mind and think about what motivates this type of person, be it a child or adult. At the root of this person's thinking is a confidence to succeed that has fueled this person's drive to achieve success.

Therefore, the root cause of success is to think yourself into being successful. There are very few cases indeed where a person has become successful but did not think long and hard about being successful. In fact, it starts to materialize only after your thoughts intensify into action. When you visualize of better days as you lay your head on your pillow, you begin to think of ways to make that better future that you see in your mind. You should wake up every morning with a purpose. Successful millionaires go to sleep every night thinking about what they need to do to maintain their wealth and make it increase, unless your goal is to make money for others. Then your drive may be slightly different, but we will get to that later.

Going to sleep thinking about making your future better should grow from a dream to a vision and then to an idea. From these ideas, plans should be developed. The mindset cannot ever be one of laziness. The first field that you must work in and learn to navigate through quite well is your own mind, never forgetting your objective. As your ideas grow stronger, they develop into solid plans. These plans need to be nurtured. Here is where many people fall short. If you know individuals who are stuck mentally where they are, then you must realize that these are not the right people with which to share your plans. It is not because they will try to steal them, but they will work to steal something far more valuable and that is your motivation. America is a nation of consumers, with the GDP around $16.7 trillion in 2014. There is plenty of money being spent on products. Unfortunately, most of the products that Americans spend their hard-earned money on are not made in America, and thus most of the labor is done elsewhere. That means the entrepreneurial bug is not very prevalent. Although we spend a lot of money, we do not produce nearly as much as we should. When the average joe who is working to pay the bills and live relatively comfortable says to his wife that he wants to start his own business, her first thought may not be to encourage him to take the risk of starting a business when he is already making money to support the family. His idea could create the next billionaire by providing a service, but it never leaves the ground floor because he tells his idea to a person who kills his spirit.

I do not mean to take shots at the wife, who is concerned about maintaining a comfortable way of life. My point is to address how ideas never develop because they are told to the wrong person, whether it is a spouse, relative, or friend. If you do not nurture your ideas in the right environment, you can set yourself up to fail. It is important that you be a leader with your ideas and plans. Learn to be self-motivated and to not be swayed easily by others. That is the only way you will succeed in business. Learn to be fierce and fearless with your ideas; develop them into plans and believe that they will succeed. Allow no one to deter you from your path, and you will succeed. Wake up every morning with a plan, and reevaluate periodically to ensure that you're not pursuing a pipedream but that you have developed realistic dreams, ideas, and plans. Dylan Smith and Aaron Levie bounced entrepreneurial ideas off each other. Smith finally came up with "digital storage," and when they needed money, they cold called a "couple of billionaires." They finally got billionaire Mark Cuban, owner of the Dallas Mavericks. Smith offers these words to the aspiring entrepreneur: "It's important to sell yourselves as much as the service. The business model's going to change 50 times and the market's going to change, but you need to convince that investor that you're smart enough and excited enough about the opportunity that you'll figure it out."[7]

The first step to achievement is the belief that you can do it. Second is an attitude that can convince others you can achieve it. Do not be swayed by the negative comments of those who may wish to cast doubt in your mind. Not only must you be self-motivated, but you must also surround yourself with people who will motivate you to do better things. Eddie C. Brown was a money manager and industry trailblazer who became the first African American money manager with the firm T. Rowe Price. He and his wife of forty-nine years have used their fortune to help many causes, donating more than $22 million to several charities, from arts to education and health care in impoverished communities. Price says this when speaking of talent and money: "I'm more concerned about keeping this exceptional talent that we have attracted and keeping the firm growing and focused than I am about another few million dollars personally."[8]

Motivation can be your greatest asset to have in life as you seek to accomplish anything. It will move you toward achieving whatever it is you want. Lacking motivation will keep you languishing. I have been motivated throughout my life to build a better future for myself and my family. At the beginning, I made the wrong decisions that were very costly to me and many others. The lesson? Although we may be motivated to accomplish something that may be noble, if we go about achieving this with the wrong idea, thus developing plans that may be harmful not only to yourself but also to others, we can end up worse off than we started.

We cannot haphazardly have ideas on success and wealth, because we may acquire it and not be fully prepared for it. Michael Steinhardt was an extremely talented hedge fund manager, making himself and others hundreds of millions of dollars in the 1990s. Looking back at his work as a power broker on Wall Street, he reminiscences, "Having grown up in a lower middle class Jewish neighborhood in Brooklyn, I didn't know what to do with all this money. It didn't interest me, all this money. What interested me was to be the best manager, doing the best job, achieving the best rates of return for my investors."[9]

Having good intentions but bad results is a path that must be avoided. Mistakes are bound to occur while on this road, but you have to work toward looking as far into the future as possible, factoring in all possible pitfalls or twist of fortune that may cause you to miss out or not maximize your potential. To bring out your full abilities, you may need to bump your head a few times. This must not discourage you from your pursuits. It will take a strong will to overcome the many obstacles that lie ahead on the road to becoming a self-made millionaire. However, the biggest one can be how you look at the obstacle itself.

Take every challenge as an opportunity to prove your worth. The battle-scarred millionaires are tried and tested. They are not where they are by accident. They did not inherit their wealth. They fought blood, sweat, and tears to get to the top. The climb becomes the test, and it also becomes the reward. It may seem from those looking on that the millionaires on top are at the best place in their lives. Talk to the millionaires themselves, however, and you will get a different story. Passing the test does become the victory. But you quickly learn that one test or struggle leads to another.

Millionaires are beset with many challenges once they become successful. Most important is how to remain successful, thus giving way to more tests. After so many struggles, you will find that successful people are driven by the very struggles that they seem to be trying to overcome. Thereby, the journey itself becomes the goal to constantly improve and struggle. The best example for this would be the art of exercises. Working out is a constant struggle, yet the end of this struggle is to be of benefit both mentally and physically. Although you get in better shape the more you work out, it is never enough. You end one day only to work on a different body part the next. You take time to rest, but it is only designed to prepare you for your next round of struggle. At the end of each session, you feel refreshed. Your body and your mind thank you. The reward itself becomes the struggle. The successful ones are those who fall in love with the pain. I know some of y'all are hating me right now, but it is the pain that leads to the reward that comes later. Therefore, you must love the process. It becomes an ongoing struggle where the reward is a good, healthy, and body.

With business, the struggle is to overcome many obstacles that come before you. The ones that drains you the most, killing morale, can be the effects of negative thinkers who secretly want you to fail. Once you discover that they are among your group or in your company, you must safeguard the body from this poison. Here are a couple of pointers. First, know that you have a responsibility to keep your group productive, and there will always be at least one person in that group whom you have offended. You may not be aware of this offense. At the root of this person's feelings is envy. Therefore regardless of what you do, I assure you that these types of people will find offense in something, and they will seek to divide the group by planting seeds among others in the group. Oftentimes you will not be aware of this until the serpent is ready to strike, yet if you pay close attention, you will find hints of the chaos that is brewing underneath the surface. Your job is to maintain morale, but because you cannot be in all places at once, you have to establish group activities that will help you sniff out your detractors. That may potentially hinder growth of your company. As a business owner or manager of business, you must be shrewd in your tact. Put projects together to motivate your group. Listen closely to them and present ideas that need to be developed. Humble yourself and even appear to be a bit unaware of something that you may be speaking of. The one who seems to take the most pride in upstaging you bears close watching. You should not take a malicious approach to this person, but you're running a business. If people are not for the team, then you have some decisions to make. You should not go about the business of firing people at whim, but you must put the business before anything and anyone. If you discover a person who seems to take pride in making you look bad in the midst of the group, then you must pay close attention to this person. This attitude cannot spread to other employees, or you will have a mutiny on your hands.

You should have a healthy relationship with your employees, especially if your business is not very large. With a larger corporation, you must have a solid team. Whenever we witness major corporations fall, it is usually the result of three things: the product is no longer in demand, the product is not longer being marketed to the correct audience, or leadership has broken down. The third one usually can be fixed the easiest. If an alert board of directors catches the problem quickly enough, before the company is totally absorbed with the infection, thereby killing morale. If corrections are made (usually a change in leadership), the company can be saved. With a smaller business, however, the politics are more subtle, but it still affects production and must be surgically removed. Start by either quickly isolating the problem or professionally removing it. Morale must remain high, and the team must be constantly motivated.

The facilitation of your rise in the company from an employee prospective is in your willingness to be a team player. Knowing how to function well on the team, playing your role well, and assisting others to ensure the team wins is a sure way to get recognition from your boss. You should develop the attitude of wanting to see the company win. If you're not currently in a field that you love and view as a career choice, you can still develop important qualities to prepare for your chosen field. How you feel about your work will make all the difference. This is also true with relationships. Your attitude will shape your overall performance. If you're unhappy with your mate, you may not put your all into the relationship. Your failure to not put forth your best effort in building and maintaining your relationship will inevitably produce a response from your mate that will likely lead to a breakdown in the relationship. This same principle applies to work: for every effect, there is a cause that produced that effect; for every action, there is an opposite and equal reaction.

Although we are dealing with mindset, this law of nature cannot be ignored. From the richest person in the world to the vagabond on any street in America, there is a story behind both, and there are valuable lessons to be learned from both. It could be argued that the root cause of one's successes and the others failures is motivation.

Cause and effect. Something has caused the billionaire to work, assumingly rather hard. The effect is that she is successful. Conversely, something has caused the vagabond to give up on hard work and resort to begging others or sifting through others trash to find a meal or something warm to wear. The effect is that he is very unsuccessful. Consequently, both principals have choices and abilities. Most people will not be reduced per se to the status of a vagabond or may not necessarily rise to the level of a billionaire. There are no set limits either way to how high or low a person can go. Your ascension or your decent will depend on you, the choices you make, the people you choose as your friends, the choices you make in terms of employment, and your education. It is all up to you and how motivated you are to achieve your life's dream. Just do it!

CHAPTER 4

Discipline

Discipline is the bread and butter of success. History is replete with examples of successful people who failed because they lacked or lost discipline along the way. Drug abuse, alcoholism, and out-of-control spending are critical road blocks to prolonged, sustained success. More money is often viewed as an access to excess. The more money you have, the more things you have to spend it on. Once you have everything you want, then the law of excess takes over the mind. This spending habit can become as addictive as any drug and often leads people to, if not into the poorhouse, then at least confining them to a reduced state of living based on the lack of discipline.

Discipline is a science, and as such it should be understood not only in its most basic term but also at its most complex level. Human nature compels us to explore, and adventuring toward the unknown is captivating to the human psyche. Yet to do so without some degree of control and reservation leads to devastating results as well as untold riches. Rest assured that riches are maintained only with discipline. Be that as it may, our goal is to first understand the mindset necessary to acquire riches and then go on to develop the skills necessary to keep and enjoy our hard-earned wealth.

That being the case, let us look at what discipline is and why it is so important. To the trained eye, this principle may seem elementary. But if you were to look at your examples, those who helped you to join in the millionaires club, as well as those who have lost their membership, you will surely discover a step-by-step process that led those both up and down the ladder of success. Let us start at the bottom and work our way to the top. At the lowest rung of the economic ladder in America, we will find a common attitude and typical activity that is recurrent in their environment.

Travel through the ghettos of America, and for those who have not developed the discipline to pick themselves up by their boot straps there is a common thread: laziness. Although this is not designed to offend anyone, it is necessary to understand this mind. It may be easy to blame the unemployment rate, but this is offered only as an excuse. America's worst cities in America are at about 10–15 percent unemployment rate. This certainly indicates that in some cities, it may be difficult to get a job. However, this does not in any way excuse those who have the ability to go out and find employment in other cities.

Detroit, Michigan, may be near the top regarding its unemployment rate. Yet those who are highly motivated have very little trouble finding a job. The easy way out is an excuse that some use to keep themselves at the bottom. Thus, from this outlook you will also find high rates of drug addiction, thereby eliminating this group from finding gainful employment until they clean themselves up from drugs, which becomes increasingly harder as the days go by. That puts this group into a permanent underclass due to their own actions. From this element, crime becomes rampant—robberies, thefts, drug selling, rapes, and murders most commonly occur among this group. They fill the prison systems because of their lack of willingness to be gainfully employed. Unfortunately, it is this group who screams the loudest about unfair treatment.

However, the root cause of all the problems mentioned is a lack of discipline leading to a life of destruction and in some cases death.

Discipline has many definitions. The ones we are after are those designed to improve.

> Order and control—a controlled orderly state

> Calm, controlling behavior—the ability to behave in a controlled and calm way even in a difficult or stressful situation

> Conscious control over lifestyle—mental self-control used in directing or changing behavior learning something or training for something. To make yourself act or work in a controlled or regular way.[1]

As we climb to the middle of the ladder, we find a relatively different mindset and a far more different environment. The first immediate, noticeable difference is in the very environment itself. The bottom of the ladder is filled with dirty streets, a large volume of broken glass, trash, abandoned houses, and a general "I don't care attitude," thus maintaining a destitute environment. Those seeking a better life for themselves and their families are forced to leave this environment, because the prevailing attitudes prevent constructive advancement without the worry of being victims of some sort of crime. The remarkable discovery here is the attitude of some who have found contentment in this environment, satisfied to wait for government relief that comes once a month. This gives those with the mindset of a temporary feeling of success. Yet there is no intention to save any of this money. Not only is there a rush to spend this money, but within two or three days, the relief money is gone, and the remainder of the month is spent waiting for the next month on whatever day the relief kicks in again. It is certainly not my intention to judge those who have relegated themselves to this type of existence. I am simply addressing the mindset of those who wish to remain at the bottom. Any similarities to any reader are not a coincidence. I come from this environment, and thus I know it all too well. My goal is to offer insight into this mindset, pure and simple. If anyone is offended, please look at your life and fix it. This is not meant to hurt any feelings.

At the middle of the ladder, we will find a change of environment, as well as a noticeable change in mindset. First, crime is not as rampant. The streets are clean, and a large percentage of the residents are homeowners. America's bread and butter resides in the middle. These are some of the most beautifully spirited people, and they have a zest for life. The neighborhoods are clean. Here, your neighbor may shovel your snow for you or cut your grass just to be neighborly. If you see a piece of paper on your neighbor's grass while you're strolling by, you may pick it up to keep the neighborhood looking nice. Here, we also find people getting up for work daily, keeping some type of order to life. They exercise the principle of discipline to some extent and call it being responsible. To these go a large amount of credit for keeping America and the world moving. Many in this class display degrees of discipline, but they do not necessarily desire to be in the millionaires' club. Although a large number of them are lottery players hoping for that big break, there is still a general contentment. The attitude of reaching for the stars is typically not present among this group. However, most millionaires start from here as well. So much is to be learned from the middle-class lifestyle. Most important among this group is education, which is encouraged. Thus, the parents of a large segment of middle-class children have hopes that their children figure out the puzzle and make it to the top. The rules to the game of money are understood to some extent and practiced. At this point, those who have ambitions of making it to a higher state of existence begin to study the money principles. To this end, let us take a bit of insight from some billionaires. Mark Cuban has some insightful words on this issue during an interview he gave to a newspaper: "You have to keep grinding. There are no shortcuts, you have to keep learning about your business, yourself and your industry, and play to your strengths. The secret is that there is no secret to success."[2]

For those seeking riches, at the point that we start thinking clearly about how we are to acquire this wealth, we then begin to look for the tools necessary to achieve this end. It is here that we begin to understand the mechanism of money making and the principles necessary to become a millionaire. This graduating process has many degrees to it. With each degree comes some difficulty that may not seem apparent by looking at the lives of many millionaires, because they seem to have it together. However, the road is rarely easy, where the flow of money is fluid and you can draw large amounts to yourself. It will only come in large amounts when you understand its principles. In an interview with the *New York Times*, Bill Gates advises, "Spending money intelligently is as difficult as earning it."[3]

One of the keys to spending money is to recognize the "need versus want" principle. With a gross domestic product of $16.7 trillion in 2014, America has a lot of spending power. With this comes plenty of frivolous spending—buying things because we like them and think they look good, but they do not necessarily serve any real purpose. Although the beauty and joy of making money is to be able to spend it on the things we want and may not need, there is certainly a place for this. Hell, life is short! If you work hard all week, you deserve to buy yourself or those you love something nice. Money is nothing if you can't spend it on the ones and things you love. Of course, that is part of the purpose of making money. Yet how many of the things we buy do we wish we hadn't, and we later felt like we wasted money that could have been best spent elsewhere? We have all felt this at some point, so the goal is to become intelligent spenders. This is not to take away any of the small things that make life so beautiful.

However, if your goal is to reach the top of the ladder, the first thing that must be established is the discipline of your pocket. Once you develop the discipline to control your spending, one thing should happen immediately: more income. More income is the first indicator that you have your money under control. When you can carefully control what goes out and keep part of what comes in, then you're on the right road. The key to being rich is learning to save. This habit will do several things for you, some of which is covered in chapter 9, but suffice it to say, it gives you a level of comfort in having money without being in a rush to spend it. Once you do decide to part with some of your money, you will do so with a small degree of reservation in most cases, but a large degree in others. There is indeed a need to keep money circulating, but you must build a nest egg and constantly work to put money away. Planning for your retirement is critical during your career.

Look forward to the future progressively, planning each stage. Although the early stages may be difficult, use it as training and preparation for a life of successfully managing money to ultimately become wealthy. You must plan. In the book *The Millionaire Next Door: The Surprising Secrets of America's Wealthy*, Drs. Thomas J. Stanley and William D. Danke share some light on wealth: "How do you become wealthy? Here, too most people have it wrong. It is seldom luck or inheritance or advanced degrees or even intelligence that enables people to amass fortunes. Wealth is more often the result of a lifestyle of hard work, perseverance, planning and most of all, self-discipline."[4]

Here at the start, we observe the importance of discipline. Another quotable from one of our honored class of billionaires comes from billionaire Don Hankey, who says, "If you wait until you need cash to get cash, it's too late."[5] Herein lies a key ingredient in both discipline and vision:

> Planning: Inside of planning, there are essentials tools necessary to become successful. First, there is vision, which we covered in chapter 1. From the vision, we start to develop ideas. From these ideas, we get motivated to achieve our visions and ideas. And from this we develop plans and goals. The act of creating sound plans and setting realistic goals puts you on the road to riches and success. There is a method to how you should set goals, discussed in more detail in chapter 7. Know here that the beginning of every successful endeavor started with a plan. From this plan, goals are set to accomplish the plan.

The difficulty with planning is not found in the plan itself but with the execution of it. As with anything worth any value, it is attendant with hardships. This struggle separates the true blues from the pretenders. Starting a company does not simply come about based on hopes and dreams. Think about the number of people who talk about their desire to do something wonderful. Some go so far as to detail plans on how they will attain the successes they envision, but this is where it stops. They have no actual goal setting or method regarding how they're to achieve this. The plans are usually choked out by the cares of this world. Either life's struggles are too overwhelming, or the follow-through is not consistent and slowly fizzles out. The primary reason why people do not follow through with their goals, dreams, and desires lies here, as well as the potential of successfully becoming a millionaire. So important are the acts of setting goals that your chances of achieving anything in life are greatly diminished by the lack of goal setting.

In setting goals, you should always have two things in mind: goals that can be reached in a reasonably short time, and those that will take time presumably several years to achieve. Each goal should be established with a solid plan to reach them. For example, if you want to find a job making more money, the first thing you must do is develop a resume highlighting your talents. If you find that you need to develop more refined skills to achieve this goal, then you must combine both short- and long-term goals—that is have the short-term goal of obtaining training or education necessary to achieve long-term goals. Thus, while you're engaged in your training and education, another component within yourself must be at play: preparation for the things that you're currently being trained for.

For anything that comes into your life, if you're not prepared to receive it, then by virtue of not being ready, you will lose it. Here, the saying "To whom much is given much is required" has its place. When you're given something, you also have with that gift a burden of responsibility. The responsibility first is to be able to handle the thing properly. With most products come instructions on how to use them. The instructions given to you must come from you being aware of what you have and what it was intended for. Failure to use it for its intended purpose will cause you to lose it and perhaps injure yourself and others. Preparation is critical to all goals for which you strive.

From this, we'll learn very important lessons already understood by most millionaires. The difference between the haves and the have-nots again rest in the understanding of this principle. First, you work hard for what you have. This work is both a physical exertion and a mental discipline. Both started with goals sustained by continuous mental imaging and preparation. As you achieve your initial goals, you set more and continue to prepare and accept your upward climb. The have-nots refuse to continually prepare themselves for advancement, so they simply do not advance.

Preparatory measure is defined as "something done in advance in order to be ready for a future event."[6] Let us resolve here that there are a very few overnight self-made millionaires. It is a process that is deliberate and takes time. Although you could sell an idea and appear to instantly become a millionaire, the time and effort it took to develop the idea is a whole story by itself. Every millionaire has a story to tell, and we would be wise to listen. In those stories are lessons that we will discover through an in-depth study, and there is a similar theme among most of them. Although there are indeed thousands of different scenarios, a common theme can be found at the root of most millionaires' climb: Thoughts at the earliest times of their rise. Motivation and service. Motivation to improve their lives. A resolution to provide some form of service to the public that can become profitable and improve the lives of others.

When setting goals, perhaps set them in a pyramid fashion. Start with mental imaging on your goals and what you will need to achieve them. Look at the base of the pyramid as the foundation you use to build your goals. From this, set step-by-step goals on how to accomplish them. Understand that you must be realistic. Having ideas on the perfect life may seem wonderful to build, but being realistic is key to becoming successful. Idealism can be fuel, yet you need to base your plans on sound practical actions.

Step 1: What are my goals?

Step 2: What do I need to achieve my goals?

Step 3: How do I get them?

This is the foundation of your pyramid, and each element discipline is necessary. Without having discipline and standing firmly on its principles, we may flounder.

CHAPTER 5

Persistence

It is discipline that will bring order and a sense of organization to your plans and goals, but persistence is the force behind the discipline. It is necessary to have it to see beyond the pitfalls and snares that must come about in your pursuit of wealth and success. It is here also where you earn your bones. Some look at persistence as a continuous pursuit of something, but there is another aspect that deserves attention.

What is that feeling deep down inside that has been lurking in your mind for many years? Part of the reason that you're reading this book comes from this longing. Where does it come from? What has equipped the human being to overcome tremendous adversity and refuse to give up? Some of the greatest champions that we have ever seen have overcome tremendous odds. Although this study is one of the millionaire mindset, we are looking mainly at the self-made millionaires, the majority of whom are first-generation millionaires. From this study, we have discovered a pattern that is present among all of them. At the forefront of this pattern is the mindset discussed in this chapter. Let us start with a quote from one of our prestigious members of the billionaire club. Ron Baron from Baron Capitol has this to say about perfecting the art of being successful: "You need 10,000 hours of practicing to be good at anything, there are no short cuts."[7]

Is there a simple, clear-cut way to become a part of the successful class in America or the world? Yes, but only if you're willing to put in the work and make the sacrifices necessary to be a part of this class.

Rest assured that America is truly the land of opportunity, but she shows no mercy to the unprepared. She devours those who put forth ideas without preparation. The reason is that there are far too many chances to learn how to properly present yourself to the world. There cannot be any mercy shown to the person who wastes the precious time of others. Thus, you cannot simply request something and expect it to come to you, unless you join the ranks of the daily consumer. To be a producer requires rigorous planning, preparation, and timing. If your product is not on time, you must continue to work to bring your product up to the modern times. America is a country that continues to advance. So much intelligence is found here that it is hard to keep up. Push your creativity to new bounds and bring something to the market that will make life easier for the average everyday consumer. One of our champions offers these timely words of encouragement to the aspiring entrepreneur. Let us take these wise words to heart. Here is a passage from NFL Super Bowl champion quarterback Drew Brees.

> In a lot of ways entrepreneurship is just creativity. Nothing is too crazy of an idea if you have the vision and desire and work ethic to put it together. You need the perseverance to get told it's a crazy and get knocked down and continue to believe in what you're trying to put together. If you ask the most highly successful entrepreneurs, there

are plenty of times people told them their ideas wouldn't come to fruition, and look at them naw. I think everybody starts at that point. That entrepreneurial mind-set teaches so many great lessons.[1]

Let us look at the lessons and learn from another giant who became one of the richest men in America and advanced the country, helping to make it a superpower among other nations in the world.

John D. Rockefeller Sr. was the son of a peddler. He started as a clerk in a small produce firm at age sixteen. At twenty-three, he entered the oil business, which was very disorganized. Rockefeller set out to make the industry orderly and efficient. Fifteen years later, he achieved his goal, and by 1882 Rockefeller controlled all US oil refining and distribution for much of the world's oil trade. His company became so powerful that the United States Supreme Court stepped in and ordered the company dissolved because it controlled too much of the country's oil supply.[2]

Mr. Rockefeller had a vision not necessarily to simply control a market in America but to build an empire that his family could benefit from many generations later. He was also a great philanthropist, donating over $520 million as well as establishing a university helping to advance the education of America. Mr. Rockefeller did his work in the late 1800s, but today his actions and his mindset are still worthy of study. He had one son, John D. Rockefeller Jr., and five grandsons, all of whom engaged in charitable works, including education, and politics to help advance America. Mr. Rockefeller is the embodiment of the millionaire mindset under study. Although some may have called a few of his tactics ruthless, history has recorded his actions honorably, and his service to America has been proven worthy of honor by up-and-coming or aspiring millionaires. The spirit of ruthlessness has its place in the competitive world of business. Be sure that if you enter this endeavor with a soft heart or mind, you will not make it far. Ruthlessness and cold-blooded shrewdness must be ever present in your mind to make it in the business world. To that end, you must learn from the best, going back to those who helped establish the country and break from the rulership of a violent dictator, King George III. We can find in the Declaration of Independence a resolve from a group of citizens who were fed up with the treatment they were under and saw greater things for its citizenry that could be experienced only when they were free from the tyranny they were under. Despite the threat of war, these brave men banded together and openly declared their independence, as well as the independence of the thirteen colonies from this tyrannical government. Certain that such action would lead to war, they overcame all internal and external opposition, went to war, and fought and bled. Some died standing on principles that "all men are created equal. That they are endowed by their creator with certain unalienable rights. That among these are life, liberty and the pursuit of happiness."[3]

It is because of the persistence of our founding fathers that we are allowed to enjoy these freedoms. We're able to enjoy a life of wealth and affluence, if we're capable. At every step in our journey to achieve wealth and success, we should always be mindful and give honors to those who led the way for us. This appreciation should be a part of your foundation. With one eye on the future and the other on the past, one must learn the examples from those who have taught us priceless lessons that can be useful for our future. Our second eye should be not only on our success but also on the upward mobility of the next generation. From my studies, I've found that the most successful among us donate a large part of their wealth to the advancement of others. You too must learn the lesson and do the same. The law of free commerce has within it an unspoken rule to leave room for others to advance. Those who seek to monopolize the market become targets of antitrust laws and auditing by the government—democracy at its finest. The little guy can grow if he uses his God-given talents. The attitude of being persistent can indeed have a negative side. Although it is good to become competitive, it also brings out of use a predatory instinct that has led man to conquer the earth. Man's desire for power and control can grow to overwhelming proportions. If not checked, it can often lead to the destruction of the individual and the company that he is trying to build. Thus, persistence must be focused. Here lies the gift of advanced training as well as the value and virtue of patience.

Persistence itself is born out of the struggles to overcome a great obstacle that is viewed as being in the way of advancement. Again, in the lives of most self-made first-generation millionaires was a desire to overcome conditions that were sometimes very restrictive or adverse. From this drive to overcome these conditions, a solid mindset is built into a prevailing attitude. From this attitude, beliefs are established that are generally geared toward success but can become very destructive. Take for example the child who came up in poverty and has developed the attitude that she will overcome this environment regardless of what she has to do to overcome it. Oftentimes crime is not out of the equation. This wanting has in fact produced many criminals who could have turned out differently if caught and redirected toward more positive ventures. To decrease that effect, let us refer back to the pyramid method first mentioned in chapter 4.

After firmly establishing the base of the pyramid or foundation of our plans to excel with the critical components of goal setting, planning, and discipline, there is another variable that must be factored into the building process: the absolute law of change. Know that everything in life changes, nothing remains the same forever, and we must be able to adapt to the changing nature of economics. As stated earlier, money is fluid, and as such it changes. The essence of money is fluid, and nothing about it is certain other than the fact that it is ever changing.

Therefore, during the goal setting and planning stages, certain factors must always be present in our minds. Look as far as you can into the future and ask questions. How long can this last? Should I base my long-term goals on this market, or must I look elsewhere? The fluidity of Wall Street can be frightening to the onlooker, making them fearful to invest any hard-earned money into such a fluid market. Your stock is up today and down tomorrow based on a news report or a financial report, someone being hired or fired. Studying the ground floor of Wall Street can be very nerve-racking. Yet hundreds of millions of dollars are traded daily on this floor. Those who decide to stay and learn this process witness the flow of money at such an alarming rate that it is mind-boggling. It is best, however, to learn this process and seek advice from professionals about investment options. The first step for the beginner, however, is not to be found on the floor of Wall Street. By the time you make it there, you hit the ground running. The beginning has to follow the proverbial steps of crawling before you walk, learning first to take your emotions out of money. This is discussed in detail in chapter 8. Regardless of our age, we must develop a grown-up approach to money management, starting always with spending habits.

America is constantly being programmed to be consumers. We must learn how to be informed consumers, but millionaires go a step further and study the thinking habits of the consumer market to find their niche. This helps start the process of deprogramming ourselves from consumer to producer. We begin to organize our minds in a way that makes us serviceable. Thus, consumers have the mindset of being served and catered to; they're willing to pay for this service. The majority of Americans go to work and earn money so that they can be serviced in some way, from the three basic essentials of food, clothing, and shelter to entertainment and luxuries. The majority of the country works to be able to afford these amenities.

The business minded, on the other hand, go to work to provide one of the services that the majority of the people will need or want. Therefore, the more people you can get to pay for your service, the more money you make. Herein lies part of the secret to success and wealth. Bruce Greenwald, finance professor at Columbia Business School, has stated a simple yet important technique for success: "First you have to be very concentrated, develop an expertise like many entrepreneurs."[4]

Developing our expertise requires first a somewhat distanced approach to money itself. Money has to come last during the visualizing and planning stages. Other latent talents must be cultivated first. If money becomes the primary goal without self-development first, then the money may come, and you may not enjoy its full properties; see chapter 9, "The Money Principle." Development of self is a part of the grand scheme to make money. As such, money is not the most important factor—you are! Cisco Systems CEO John Chambers has sat atop of a multi-billion-dollar company for nearly two decades, and he offered these words in *Forbes* on self-development: "I have to constantly reinvent myself, if you don't do that you get left behind."[5]

One must be persistent, focused, and determined. If there is a key to becoming successful, the key would simply be designed to unlock these qualities within oneself. Unleashing our dormant talents frees us to soar to great heights. With this in mind, we may find that the biggest obstacles to our future advancement and success may well be ourselves—the thoughts we have become so accustomed to that can hinder us in so many ways and that we may not even be aware of.

I am not espousing a great scheme to keep the majority blind and happy. We can argue that the majority has simply grown comfortable in the middle. The process is not quick; it may likely take some years to realize a goal of wealth and success. Disappointment is certain along the way. It will seem at times that people are truly standing in the way of your advancement. At these critical points, it is very important that we still look within. Regardless of what someone does to possibly interfere with our success, if our focus remains clear, we can overcome them.

Usually at times like these, when someone seems to be standing in our way, our first reaction is emotional, primarily anger. How we express our emotions can determine our next steps and the following consequences. The best reaction in the face of an opponent is no reaction at all. Do all you can to settle the turmoil you feel and continue to push forward. Oftentimes we will find that our first reaction to a situation may not be the best one. Once we settle down, we can then see our potential opponent with more clarity. If we take the time to carefully study our opponents in business, we can discover two critical points. First, you will be able to possibly detect why you're being opposed. Either there is something wrong with your plan, approach, or something else—or they're against you because you're right on target, and they do not wish to see you advance. For the former issue, you must take the time to rearm yourself, learning valuable lessons from your opposition. To do this, you should humble yourself and seek advice for improvement from the people who appear to be against you. From this, you may develop an ally who could possibly help you go on to success.

For the latter, you must politely maneuver around them, being careful not to be offensive if possible. Under no circumstances, however, are you to let this type of people hold you back. They have found a fault in you that will keep them against you. Do not waste any time reasoning with them or trying to befriend them. They may have an infectious personality that could be fatal to your career. Learn to stay away from them at all cost. If you must deal with them, or you have such type as your boss, do not let them wear you down. They will constantly work to diminish your flare to take away some of your brightness.

Learn the art of passive aggression and declare a subtle war against this type. In your warfare, learn to totally disengage your emotion. Become completely numb emotionally but totally alert mentally. For example, do not wear your feelings on your sleeve. Detach yourself from the emotions of yourself, and you will not feel the attacks of your boss. You remain completely alert so that your work performance will remain intact. This mental outlook can prepare you for the corporate world. But in the realm of small business you must be more engaged with your clients. This type of mental fortitude is indeed necessary throughout the business world. We will also be faced with difficult customers. At no time are we to ever lash out at customers. Regardless of their words, we must always remain professional. When dealing with a large customer base, security may sometimes be necessary.

During my experience working for a housing commission, I had the privilege of working with an extremely professional supervisor. My supervisor happened to have a small sign on his door that read "Tough Guy." Every day, my supervisor was the first to arrive at work, at times with doughnuts, and he was the last to leave. Because our job dealt with public housing, he often dealt with angry, irate people. He never seemed angry and always did all he could to accommodate the resident. He showed me that toughness was found not in one's ability to do damage but how much one could endure from others and not lose one's decorum. Take it from Super Bowl champion Drew Brees as he discussed NFL strategies on winning: "When you start a season, every year is a new year regardless if you have veteran players. Circumstances change, things change. It's a new year every year. You know your competition is getting better as well. At the beginning of each year you work to put that team together. You work to figure out the dynamics, you work out how you're going to piece it together and put everybody in the best position to succeed, just like you do with a business. Everybody has a specific role in order to make the business go. You know there are going to be bumps along the way. There's going to be adversity, but you know its going to make you stronger, going to make you better. You have to fight, through it, move forward, get knocked down, get back up."[6] That sounds like the making of a true champion to me.

Speaking on the engaged mind in the competitive world of business, the art of warfare is truly necessary. From the most successful people in business to the world of politics, the art of civil warfare is essential, although you do not declare war on your competitors per se. The art of winning is broken down the same way as strategies for war. First, you must train. While in physical war, you train and prepare for combat. In financial wars, the training is mental. Preparation comes from information and technology. Depending on the market, this information includes detailed intelligence on a competitor—not to undermine their products but to beat them to market or decide on alliances called mergers.

Leaders of the industry surround themselves with able soldiers who offer sound advice on how to develop the best strategies and introduce a product to the market or the public. These companies do their hiring based on the potential aggressiveness of a prospective employee, and to this end, preparation for the new recruit is based on either high grades on particular test scores or success in the financial arena. Likely candidates for the more affluent businesses come from Ivy League colleges such as Harvard School of Business, Wharton School of Business, and others. Do not be dismayed if you did not matriculate from one of these prestigious schools, even though they do indeed have a high success rate. The majority of self-made millionaires did not come from such schools. Some of the most successful either dropped out of college or did not go. The benefit of having a persistent spirit is that you overcome all obstacles. You do not let anyone tell you that you have to come from a certain school or followed a particular path to make it. To a large degree, you make your own rules. You have told yourself that you're going to be successful, and you tolerate nothing else. You program yourself to win, and you do not rely on what someone else tells you, or what someone else said you cannot do. This is discussed in detail in chapter 7.

The second strategy in business that is likened unto war is marketing or propaganda. In war, you have to affect the minds of the enemy troops, lowering their morale and lifting the spirit of your own soldiers—esprit de corps. Also, with a successful war, the government spreads propaganda to generate support from the people to enliven the soldiers and turn the hearts of the country against the common enemy, real or imagined.

In business, the goal is different, but the strategies are in essence the same. To market to an audience, you must first learn their likes and dislikes. From this critical information, you develop advertising committees that put together ads and other tools to catch the attention of the public. Millions are spent on marketing a product to the potential consumer. In marketing strategies, several components are necessary to study, and not only likes and dislikes. In fashion, food, and other markets, timing is also important. If you catch the people at the wrong time with your product, you could miss them—for instance, marketing winter accessories in the middle of the summer, or advertising dinner food at breakfast time. You have to be in tune with the people and be up to date with your service. Thus, while most are resting, you're busy fine tuning yourself to present the most feasible product. Your persistence will always pay off.

CHAPTER 6

Cooperation

Now that we have developed ourselves enough to grow keenly aware of our own talents and abilities, we must focus our energy on building the proper network of people. Learning how to function well in a group is vital in becoming successful. You cannot become wealthy on your own. It is for the most part very unlikely that we will ever attain any high place without the aid and cooperation of others. Therefore, it is incumbent that you start early picking out a team and building good rapport with all of them.

Cooperation is defined as "The act of working together to achieve a common aim."[1] In business, we have cooperatives established that are designed to create harmonious businesses by allowing individuals with similar interest and products to pool their resources and become a larger entity, creating a surplus of goods provided at wholesale prices to smaller businesses. To create cooperatives is a good example of businesses working together.[2]

In pursuit of wealth and providing service, there must be various forms of organization, starting first with the control of emotion and learning the art of visualization. From this we begin to develop ideas and goals. With the goals must come some degree of order and control. It has been said that the first law of the universe is motion, and the second law is order. Thus, everything set in motion must be brought under order. We find this order through a system of rules and structure. Before we can manifest our visions and ideas, we must ensure that they are well thought out and properly developed.

We gain understanding into the viability of our plans, and once we accept that it is a viable plan, we must then look at strategies. How do we make this work? Whom do we need to help us make this become a reality? What are the programs that we need to make this work? Here is another step in the ladder—another key in the process, if you will. Whether you're the manager of a company or starting your own business, if you're still going through the educational process (college, training, etc.), you will need a team, a network of reliable, proficient individuals that will help you move upward. Let us look at some wise words from one of our greatest, Bill Gates, captain of the billionaires' club with a net worth of $76 billion: "You need a strong team, because a mediocre team gives mediocre results, no matter how well managed it is."[3]

Your selected personnel can make or break your company. In choosing strong, competent people, what are some of the most important qualities to look for? Attitude, attitude, attitude. Finding people who are extremely talented but have bad attitudes can be worse than finding a person who is not as talented but has a good attitude. From a manager's prospective, ability can only take you so far. Talent is very valuable if you have a talented person as your, say, chief of operations. But if the person is not very motivated, he or she may produce work that is subpar, as well as not be very inspirational to other subordinates. Conversely, take a manager who does not have the advanced education and qualifications of the chief of operations but who has garnered the talent of motivating the employees to do exceptional work.

The company would clearly thrive more under the latter example despite the person not having the education.

Millionaires possess a key quality necessary in production, and that is simply the right attitude. Part of your job in helping to build a solid structure within your company is to be vigilant of the changing in attitude and how it relates to work performance. Being a leader requires that you wear many hats. One of them is to be available as a counselor and supporter of your employees. It is not always about the bottom line.

Your employees are human beings, and are all susceptible to various emotions and problems depending on what may be going on in their lives. Part of the reason of your making yourself available to your employees is to understand the people you have working for you. If you find yourself to be the type who is only concerned with the bottom line, then you will need to hire someone to get in the nooks and crannies of the company. Starting a new venture means that all of your people are relatively fresh to each other and the politics have not taken deep roots. Start early getting to know your team. Try as much as you can to keep an open-door policy. This will work wonders to keep the company functioning on one accord.

With respect to the attitude, it can be a gauge to test the general health of the company. If there is a general attitude among the group that morale is low, then you have reached a critical point. Start by talking to people individually to see if there is a specific reason why morale is low. It may be the result of an overbearing manager who does not know how to deal with people, or it could be that you are not stimulating the group enough. Now you have to become the listener. As a leader, you must be humble in order to excel. Take the example from one of our greats from the millionaires' club:. "If you truly listen to what people are saying, you'll find out what's on their minds that they want to be comfortable with, and then you'll be more effective in addressing their concerns."[4]

You must listen to the concerns of your people. When you see a switch of morale either in a particular employee or as a group, this should set off an alarm with you, and you will need to stop what you're doing to listen to your employees and do all that you can to address their concerns. To accomplish this, regular meetings are indeed necessary to unify your team. These meetings are also required to promote growth within your company. From these meetings, you will learn to identify the leaders among your group—those who have ambition, as well as those who will ultimately require removal. So much is to be said about these general meetings. Your primary goal, however, is to ensure that everyone is aware of the team mission and mission of the company, keeping everyone on the same page and allowing for general issues to be addressed. This is also when you learn about the dispositions of your managers vis-à-vis your employees.

In order to maintain harmony, it will be necessary to periodically shake up the company to continue to stimulate growth and shake off the slackers. You may need to occasionally replace your management team and put new leadership in place. This is a delicate maneuver and should be handled very carefully. As a practice, make your management the last to go, unless there are obvious problems that can be fixed with a change of the guard. As a daily goal, try to make the work environment feel as much like a family as possible. Co-CEOs of The Roberts Bros. Properties say that to boost company morale, "We make sure that everyone here becomes family and acts like it. That is part of the genesis of our success."[5]

The type of environment that you create at work sets the tone for how the company employees will respond to you and each other.

Barbara Corcoran, the dynamic personality who successfully built her company, Corcoran Group, into the largest residential brokerage firm in New York, had some insightful words on one of the most effective ways to maintain company morale: "I found the more fun I created in the company, the more creative and innovative it became, that was the big kahuna—the fun piece. That's what built that culture upside down and inside out. You got innovation, you got loyalty, you got people who would recruit for you."[6]

Having fun does indeed create wonderful team spirit, but it must be clear that work is first. Performance should be monitored to analyze progress, both for the company and personally, on a personal note, taking regular inventory of yourself is good, from the thoughts you have to the actions you take. It is always good to keep yourself in perspective, ensuring that you're still working on your goals. In life, it is very easy to get sidetracked by other things and lose focus on what you may have started that could lead to great results.

Follow-through is an important quality that could be missing from your repertoire, preventing you from excelling. In order to develop a solid team with everyone being on the same page, we must first harmonize our own minds, learning what our different idiosyncrasies are. For instance, if you find yourself dominating conversations, you must train yourself to become more of a listener. You must first work on whatever defects you know of yourself that could possibly interfere with the team spirit.

Among most type-A personalities, being dominant is second nature. In fact, this trait is part of the reason you are where you are. However, in a group setting with other type-A and type-B personalities, we must be able to nurture the common touch. Learning how to unify your team and keep them together starts in the home and could go back as early as your own childhood. Human beings have a kinship that binds us together, and we each share common traits. Most important is the family bond. Whether or not we individually experienced this union of the family, we can relate to it. Let's hear again from Barbara Corcoran: "I never thought of it as leadership, but I know I wanted to be loved by the people who worked for me. I built the business exactly the way my mother built and ran her family. I wanted a replication of the big, happy family I grew up in. I wanted happy people having fun."[7]

In business, having alliances both within and outside of the company can be very helpful in advancing. The spirit of America embodies the importance of networking so much that a branch was created to help develop aspiring business owners into well established businesses. The reason for this has a lot to do with the interconnectedness that we have one to the other. If the government helps you develop your business then you can help to employ more Americans, helping to stimulate the economy and simply keeping the country and the world moving forward. The Small Business Administration has helped many small businesses get their start and provides not only financial startup but also counsel to the up and coming entrepreneur. In 2010, Karen G. Mills, as the head of the US Small Business Administration, had some encouraging words from the federal government regarding small business and President Barack Obama's plan to cooperate with this element of America: "In most communities we are extremely relevant to both main street small business and to the young entrepreneurs. The president has really made small business a priority, so that the SBA under President Obama has enormous support. He really understands that small business is part of the way to middle class prosperity."[8]

Before we present our plans to the world for review and assistance, we must first check all of our systems. Building a successful business is similar to building and maintaining a successful life. With every aspect of our lives, in order to become proficient, there must be some type of structure and organization. You cannot go about life and be successful getting up without a plan and a purpose. In fact, most purpose-driven people are early risers. While most people are snuggled cozily in their beds, the achiever is up and starting his or her workday. This is not usually done by force either. These people are driven from a deep sense of trying to accomplish something that they see in their minds and that compels them to act. They cannot lie around because something within them will not allow it. The most important aspect of this mindset is a systematic order of business. In life, we will always encounter different people who will, at critical times in our lives, provide us with a service that helps push us further down the road to success. These people serve a unique purpose of helping us bring out the qualities we possess that we need to accomplish our goals. Whether or not they give us sound advice or teach us a lesson that will be useful, they help us to advance on an individual level.

So too with business. People will come into your business life who embody certain qualities that you need to advance your company. The most important element of establishing your company is building a solid structure. Again, here is the US Small Business Administration's head, Karen Mills: "This is a fantastic agency and it is highly relevant to small business and to the economy. The first indication is that we were able to put $25 billion into the hands of small business over this recession and really fill part of this credit gap that existed because of the financial crisis. But, in addition, we have bone structure, a network all across this country that's extremely powerful."[9]

Structure is vital to the success of any business endeavor we get. Thus, finding the correct people is one of the most important decisions you will make concerning the future of your company. How do you go about this selection? What are some of the most important qualities you need to look for in your future employees? Once you start your business, your chain of command has to be one of the first things you establish. If it is a small business, this will start out simple. You should be present as often as possible. Your presence is needed to establish your company the way you want it run. In your absence, however, is where all the problems will occur if you have not properly trained your people. In America, every business falls under various codes of law, from the building codes to OSHA and labor laws. Every established business must operate under these laws and standards.

So important are these safety regulations that if your business is not following them, an immediate shutdown could be ordered depending on the alleged violation. Because of the rules, regulations, and laws, you must be aware of them and ensure that your second in command is also well informed about them. If you're a part of a larger company, chain of command and structure becomes even more important.

As the head of the company, you set the tone for the leadership. At the base of your leadership should be a constant observance of the Golden Rule: "Do unto others as you would have them do unto you." Simply put, treat people the way you want to be treated. How you deal with your subordinates, from your second in command to the newest hires, should always be with the general idea that you want everyone to feel good while at work. Thus, during your interview stage, look for people who have the best attitude about the job, not those who seem to be trying to impress you because they want a job. Find people who really want to work at your company. If your work will require that your employees interact with the public, you should have a range of questions concerning how to deal with people. At the top of the list should be issues regarding professionalism.

How to conduct yourself in a professional manner at all times while engaged in business involves a code of ethics dealing with both the business and the people. With business, there should always be integrity with work performance—an honest day's work for an honest day's pay. As an employee, your attitude should always be to do the work that you're expected to do, putting forth all the necessary effort to perform your work at your best. With time and focus, you will become a professional in any field that you work.

As an employer, you should always provide the best environment for your employees to work in, with the attitude of always putting yourself in your employees' shoes. If it would be something that you would have trouble doing, then do all you can to make it easier for your employees. Remember the "Golden Rule." With a clear understanding that your people help put food on your table as well as their own, bring out the best in each one of them.

One of the greatest writers of the twentieth century, Napolean Hill, espoused a principle for getting the best out of your people and creating another force from the harmonious interaction of your group to benefit the whole. He called it the Mastermind Principle. A group of two or more people cooperate together, putting their mental energies on a particular issue, which creates a third force or mind. Combining the energies of the group together creates a mastermind.[10] Once these ideas, thoughts, and suggestions are logged, they can become a conduit to propel the company forward. And with each forward step, all members of the group feel a personal sense of accomplishment because they too helped put forth these ideas.

Such is the case with the corporate board. Among the board, there is a harmony that is created that moves the entire company forward. In building a stronger vehicle, Henry Ford envisioned a more efficient car capable of using eight cylinders. He put a group of his engineers in a room and instructed them to figure it out. After many hours of brainstorming, they could not figure out a way to make the motor. They went to Henry Ford and complained to him that they could not come up with a way to make it work. Ford, confident in his vision, advised them to go back and keep trying. After more effort, they again went to Ford in frustration, and he again told them to go back and figure it out. Finally, after much mental digging, this group came up with the concept for operating a vehicle on an eight-cylinder motor. This proves the power of the mastermind principle. Put a group of people in a room with instructions on solving a problem, and they will come up with a solution.

Another example is the American system of jurisprudence, where every person accused of a crime has a right to be judged by a jury of his or her peers. This jury system has at its root the mindset that all have to agree on a verdict, or else it is deemed a hung jury. This system puts the jury in the position to where they all have to be of one mind in order to render a fair and just verdict. Having twelve jurors means that the issue should be looked at from every possible side, weighing all the evidence and making a unanimous decision. This decision, if unanimous, creates one mind among the group, and from this decision another person's fate is determined. That is a perfect example of people cooperating together, working on a single goal, and uniting all of their minds into one mind, the mastermind.

Create this type of harmony in your home, and your family will be wholesome, united, and productive. Do so at work, and you have a unit that will be effective and powerful. Whether you have a small business or a corporation, create a corporate board and run your company with that type of mentality. Once you have your chain of command, work closely with your group and develop team spirit, where each person works well with the rest of the team. This too will help in promoting others to more active roles in the company and encouraging them to work harder to essentially make room at the top for themselves. They will help you advance the cause of the company because they have a personal stake within it and want to see it thrive. They will happily help you and the team see their goals, creating both successful people individually and a prosperous company. Learning to identify potential in others and encouraging them to reach their maximum capabilities will surely advance your company. Key to this process of identification is your willingness and ability to listen closely to your people. One of the lost arts in human behavior is the art of listening. Learning how to be an effective communicator will reside in your ability to listen. Listening requires that you first detach yourself from your emotions and be able to listen without the urge to respond. Resisting the urge to respond will help you listen to not only the words being expressed but the unspoken words that lie at the root of the issue. Being a problem solver requires that we listen closely to people's issues, concerns, and complaints.

Once you have heard these issues, your response should always come after careful consideration. Sometimes your only response at the moment should be, "I will take everything you have said into consideration, and we will make all the necessary changes." Not only can these steps be helpful in creating a better work environment, but they can also help with personal relationships. The thing that most people want is to be heard and to know that their ideas matter, that people care about the way they feel, and that they're wanted and appreciated.

After all is said and done, the main thing your employees want is to know that they are appreciated. If you work to build a good team, then you will have the right people who share your commitment to the company goals, have a similar work ethic, and hopefully have a genuine love for the company as well. When you have a team like this in place, your objective should always be to show them how much you appreciate them. There is a saying: "Those who play together stay together." Not only should your employees have fun, but you should also give parties where everyone is able to reap the benefits of hard work.

Plan lavish parties around Christmastime and give gifts to all of your employees. Make a calendar with all of your employees' birthdays and be sure that everyone gets a card and possibly a cake and a small celebration on their birthdays. Invest in your people. You are surely to get a return on your investment. Have a genuine love and appreciation for your team, and they will grow to love you in return.

Cooperation within a company means that the company operates well with each member. Each member plays an important role in the advancement of the company, and all work as one body. Work to eliminate self-importance, starting first with yourself. You should not feel the need to remind people that you're the boss. Whenever discipline is necessary, be fair and just. At this point, professionalism is the key. You are as important as your team!

CHAPTER 7

The Law of Success and Failure

All life follows a pattern of evolution, from the flower that blooms to the bees that extract its elements, to the bear that hibernates in winter. Every life has a pattern, a flow that gives purpose to everything in existence. However, when it comes to human beings, we have a pattern that while one part is natural, there is another aspect that is totally based on the thoughts we carry from moment to moment. Each thought carries with it a series of actions, creating patterns and habits within our psyche that we grow comfortable with and accustomed to. From these actions, we bring upon ourselves a universal law of cause and effect.

So certain is this law that lives are built and destroyed on it without many people ever being aware of it. What you put out will inevitably come back. Although it may not yield an immediate response, the time is definitely coming where we must reap what we sow. Locked within the human mind is a logging system that stores everything that we do. It is stored, and as we continue to act in a positive or negative way, our actions are gradually building up to a return that must come about in due season.

Take for example an A student who goes through college, taking the time to learn all of the lessons that college is set up to teach. They learn not only the curriculum taught by the various professors but also the life lessons taught by being in the college environment, these actions are certain to produce the desired results. Second, if this same college student harbors positive thoughts, visions, and ideals about the future, then a promising future indeed lies ahead.

Conversely, the student who does not study well and received failing grades in classes has taken to the dark side of college life and does not listen to the professors and their wise guidance. People like this will not prosper until they change their outlook and behavior. These examples may seem simple and quite self-explanatory, but they are thinking patterns that are both constructive and destructive. Although some may not possess a completely constructive (positive) or totally destructive (negative), mind, there are elements of both in human nature.

What we need to do is develop the ability to distinguish people who have become programmed to fail and those who have programmed themselves to succeed. The core of both thought processes are within the individual.

For the person programmed to fail, there is a pattern of behavior that every employer should be trained to look for. Although it should not be the intention of an employer to eliminate people from the hiring process based on past failures, you must train yourself to identify certain types of behavior and their attendant thinking patterns.

Be advised that truly negative thinking people walk around with a poison in their bloodstream that is contagious and must be pulled out with the right antidote. Some may try to hide their negative thinking patterns behind a smile or noble intention, but be very mindful of them. Unfortunately, there is not always a quick way to identify a negative thinker and everyone can view a certain circumstance or situation negatively at the moment and not be totally negative. Although negativity is relative, a pattern of failures is a possible indication of someone who is programmed to fail.

Because of the broadness of this mindset, you will likely not notice it until some type of failure is already upon you. Here again is the purpose of regular meetings and evaluation of work performance. Ask questions to learn from your people and their various thinking patterns. Listen closely because you will learn a lot about the people you have working with you. Before we delve into the work environment, however, let us look at how this thought process takes root. Failure itself is a part of life. No one will succeed all the time at everything that he or she does. We have all experienced times when we have missed the boat. Did this when we should have done that? Did we go that way when we should have gone this way? Each bad decision, miscalculation, or negative response that we wish we had not done is attributable to our own individual frailties and shortcomings. They are natural and part of our learning experiences.

The people who feel that they have no regrets and have always made all the right decisions regardless of the outcome have yet to learn and appreciate the beauty of learning from our mistakes. It is truly our bad decisions that help shape and mold our characters to become wise, refined individuals. Despite all that, we have been told we must, as human beings, learn some lessons on our own. Life becomes more valuable to us because of our mistakes, bad decisions, and unfortunately our devastating losses.

There are people among us, however, who seem to fail to learn from their mistakes. They seem to keep going the wrong way;

regardless of how much they lose, they just cannot seem to keep it together. "One step forward, two steps back" is their motto. We also find ourselves at different times and at different stages in our lives. Thus, it is here that we study carefully the thought processes that constantly lead to failure—the mindset that we need to understand so that we can effectively work to change it.

Here resides the attitude that we must look at. What are some of the thoughts that reside at the root of failure? Foremost among them are the paralyzing emotions of doubt, fear, insecurity, and procrastination. So destructive are these emotions that we must constantly work to remove them from our thoughts as they relate to taking the proper actions.

Doubt is defined as "to be uncertain, disbelieving, or skeptical about, to lack trust or confidence in."[1] Having doubt can be natural to some extent. However, to let it interfere with your execution can be fatal to your actions. Whenever we have unjustified doubt about a person or thing, it can hinder us from acting correctly. We must learn to remove doubt by intelligent observation of both the person or thing we feel doubtful toward, as well as ourselves, This means that we must learn to process information and people quickly and place them in general categories. This is a quick process, but it must be based on facts, not feelings. In other words, unless people have given you a reason to be doubtful about them, you should not doubt them. If a reason does in fact exist, then there should be no doubt, only factual information. As a businessperson, you should develop a somewhat detached view of people. By this, I mean that you must take your emotions out of most of your encounters with people. In your emotions, there is also judgment, which may be based on many factors, some of which may be totally misguided. Intelligent observation dictates that your interaction be based on necessity. Thus, you take away doubt and put people into the category of serving some purpose.

Nothing that you do in your pursuit of wealth and success should be done aimlessly. There should be a reason and a purpose for every move that you make. When you're able to function on this vibe, you will remove doubt from your thinking.

Second on the list of emotions that can lead to failure, or at the least prevent you from utilizing your full potential, is fear. Fear is closely related to doubt because it creates a feeling of uneasiness or apprehension, leading to uncertainty or lack of trust. Fear is a very powerful emotion that can restrict our movements. How many people have left the world with tremendous talent, with gifts that could have served man well, had it not been for the people being fearful and doubtful of their own talents? How many people right now sit on valuable talents and skills, afraid to show themselves to the world because of something that someone has told them about themselves? What is at the root of fear? Doubt, plain and simple. It is doubt that someone will accept them, or fear that they will be hurt by someone. It has been said that human beings' three greatest fears are heights, the unknown, and rejection.

Let us deal with the last two, because the first one is quite obvious. We'll start with the fear of the unknown. To not know the expected outcome of some things can frighten some people. This comes from a life of comfort and predictability. We are creatures of habit, and most of us hate change. Bring something new, and it may be rejected simply because it may require us to change our normal habits. Yet entrepreneurs are innovators. Thus, fear of change or the unknown is not in the bloodstream of the business minded. So too with the next fear.

Now let's look at rejection. So powerful is this fear that people refuse to move forward and take chances because they have developed a fear of being rejected. To hurt people's ego and their sense of self-worth can be devastating to some, but entrepreneurs know that they must develop a resistance to the natural urge to withdraw because of the feeling of being rejected. They must challenge their fears and move forward with a persistent focus on the goal. Again, there is an antidote for this powerful emotion: to see in your heart a noble vision. Holding in your soul a desire to provide some form of service to your fellow man shall empower you to overcome this paralyzing emotion. Just do it and get it over with. Go get it! The word *no* is not going to kill you. It will in fact make you stronger. You have to hear some *no*s before you get to the *yes*es.

Fear creates another emotion that begins to grow and manifest itself through our personality. Insecurity starts as a fear of some sort, but if left unaddressed, it will most assuredly grow and take over your life, affecting relationships, work, and how you deal with people on a daily basis. To be insecure is to not be firm or dependable, not be confident, and be filled with anxieties. To suffer from insecurity can truly prevent our rise. There is a very simple solution to this problem: to accept yourself as you are. This does not mean that you should not work to improve your shortcomings, but you should not pity yourself for the things that you do not have or that you may see others with. Developing these negative emotions from insecurity can also lead to envy and jealousy. Stop these feelings before they grow, by simply accepting yourself. People are where they are and the way they are for a reason. Hate or dislike no one for their good qualities that you wish you possess, learn to find the good qualities you have, and work to eliminate the bad. Know that it is a process and will not come overnight. But if you remain focused on your goals to better yourself, you most certainly will. Learn to develop a love and appreciation for people, and they will see the good qualities in you.

Next on the list of actions that lead to continuous failure is procrastination. Oh, boy, here we go. An entire book can be written on the procrastinator. The least serious of all, procrastination is not rooted in an emotion but an action, or the lack there of. The root cause of it, however, is laziness. No matter what excuse we put on it, to be a procrastinator is to be lazy. It is to defer or delay something without legitimate reason. Of course, if there is a good reason for a delay, then it is simply that. Yet when we continuously put something off that we need to handle, then we have become lazy or uninterested in that particular thing.

Procrastination can be overcome with some degree of easiness by pushing ourselves to action. A suggestion for the chronically busy is to develop a to-do list and review it daily. Nothing on your to-do list should go days without being addressed. Those issues that keep coming up that may not seem important may need to be passed on for someone else to address or taken off the list altogether.

Know that each issue discussed carries with it thinking patterns that can lead to failure. They are self-defeating attitudes that have grown in our thought processes and that lead to actions, the end result of which were unsuccessful. Depending upon the depth of these thoughts will determine the extent of work necessary to overcome these destructive thinking patterns. An immediate solution is to start a complete reversal in our thought process. Failure is as deliberate as success, though not on a conscious level. We do not necessarily plan to fail, but the core of our thinking will inevitably cause us to fail if we carry with us consistent patterns of negative thinking.

There is a cause and effect law that is at play at every step of the way leading to failure (i.e., the action, then the reaction). This law is unavoidable and goes to the very root of our thinking. Reversing the thoughts creates a different dynamic.

Conversely, success is the result of concentrated positive thinking with the attitude of "I will win." There is a pattern, however, to this thinking as well. We have detailed the various principles or core thoughts that are necessary to achieve success, but there are also some dominating thoughts that carry us from moment to moment, step by step, on our way to achieving our plans and goals. These thoughts are reinforcers to ensure success and act as insulators against the ever-present thoughts and emotions that lead to failure.

Foremost among them is the foundation of faith, which is defined as "mental acceptance of the truth or actuality of something."[2] Faith is something that can be planted early in life. It can be detected in children early and will travel with them throughout life. It starts with a confident belief in the success of a parent, sibling, or other close family member. A strong belief in people that makes someone accept what others say or do as truth. From early on, faith is instilled in the child's ability to achieve something based on what it is told it can do. Make a child believe he or she will conquer the world, and that child will set out to do it. Only time and circumstances may thwart one's efforts. With persistence and constant encouragement, a solid faith both in God and themselves gives way to another equally important attribute: courage.

Now we separate the men from the boys and the girls from the women. Having faith gives you courage. Having trust that you can accomplish what you set out to do gives you the courage to go out and do it. You have the attitude that you can face and deal with anything dangerous, difficult, or painful and come out on top. Our police officers are the best examples of overt courage while providing service to the public. Their motto is to serve and protect. They drive around looking for individuals who may be a menace to the good order and the peace and safety of the public. The police address them directly without hesitation or fear. Their goal is to protect the public even if it costs them their lives. We must always acknowledge and respect the service the police provide and yield to them whenever necessary to ensure that they are not hindered in any way.

With regard to business, having courage means that you're willing to break away from the pack and go out on your own to achieve your dreams, visions, and goals. Without this critical element, many plans never come to fruition. There were times in entrepreneurs' lives when they were told that they could not do what they were thinking about and that they should forget about their dreams. Had they listened to someone else and not the longing that they felt at the core of their being, we would not have enjoyed the benefits of their services. So too with future entrepreneurs. So much lies within you that can be used by the public, but unfortunately we will never know and benefit from some of these exceptionally talented people and their services because they lack the courage to stand up and announce to the world that they have something to offer. Many businesspeople are fearless. They're unafraid to lose their entire fortune because they are confident that they will get it back if they ever lose it. That leads us to our next ingredient.

The heart of success lies right in confidence. An absolute faith in yourself and your abilities because of constant work and practice builds a confidence that makes this person successful in everything in your life. Because you believe in yourself and your abilities, things seem to happen for this person, but that is not the case. Success and failure are both largely based on the mindset—your outlook on life and your relation to it. As stated earlier in this book, "Believe you will succeed, and you will." This is so because this belief is suggestive. Let us humbly defer to one of our great ones. Mr. James Allen advised us in 1903 about the power of the mind in our ability to be successful. Let us take his words to heart and examine them carefully: "To put away aimlessness and weakness, and to begin to think with purpose, is to enter the ranks of those strong ones who only recognize failure as one of the pathways to attainment; who make all conditions serve them, and who think strongly, attempt fearlessly; and accomplish masterfully."[3]

Confidence breaks down the toughest walls, sometimes causing wars. Abraham Lincoln, the first US president assassinated, held a belief that was so strong that it caused a civil war and nearly permanently split the country. He is regarded by many as the greatest person in United States history. Despite the country being at war, Lincoln espoused a vision of America's future in which all people would have the right to rise in life. He had the courage to stand against a system that he believed would ultimately hurt America, and he felt it was against the vision of the Founding Fathers found in the Declaration of Independence. One of President Lincoln's famous quotes came before he was actually elected president: "Let us have faith that right makes might, and in that faith let us to the end dare to do our duty as we understand it."[4]

In his example, President Lincoln displayed all of the primary steps to achieve success, and under his leadership at one of the most critical times in our nation's history, he was able to unite a country, bring an end to a civil war that also started with his presidency, and bring an end to the system of slavery. Because of his actions, the character of America has matured.

In taking a closer look at many of the qualities that can lead to either failure or success, we will indeed find a link to each one while none of them are inherent in any of us. We can act them out either way, and the consequences for each is as certain. Although these things may not come natural, we are seeking here to start the process that will lead us to success and avoid the actions that can lead to failure.

A vision is truly important, and leadership helps guide and direct us on the right course. Nothing can stop a mind that is unconsciously programmed to fail by reinforced self-defeating thoughts. Regardless to the amount of education, if this programming that is found at the root of our thinking is not changed, then regardless of how much positive influence is present at the end of the day, failure will come. Therefore, we must go to the root cause and work diligently to uproot negative thinking from our minds. This is certainly not as easy as it sounds, nor does it happen quickly.

Take smokers for an example. Many people who smoke wish that they could simply stop smoking, but things are not that easy. Once the body is addicted to nicotine, then a whole different series of events takes place within the smoker's body. The body has been programmed to crave nicotine. When it does not receive it, the body starts to go through withdrawal, causing the body and the mind to make the person again yield to the nicotine. It takes a great amount of discipline and courage to stop smoking once the body becomes addicted. This courage and discipline comes with some degree of pain and mental anguish. A deprogramming is in effect, and it is not easy.

The programming for failure runs deeper than the smoker who is addicted to nicotine. But the process of training ourselves to stop negative thinking is not physically or mentally painful. It is simply a process that takes time and may likely require a change of environment. In many cases, our environment is a result of our thinking both positively and negatively. If we find ourselves in a negative environment, the moment we start to change our way of thinking, we will gradually start to see a change in our environment. So too with friends. Here is a place where we can find a lot of our negative thoughts encouraged and influenced. For example, if you wish to stop smoking, you will need to temporarily remove yourself from friends who smoke, or at least ask them to not smoke around you. However, smoking is the result of negative thinking at some point, so unless your friends who smoke also desire to stop smoking, they will probably not be encouraging, and it will be best to distance yourself for a time until you can build up your strength. The idea of success is not always shared by everyone, and because you have started to become successful, that does not mean that everyone around you will also become successful. While you are on this journey, there is a very specific reason why you must keep only the people close to you who are on their way to also becoming successful or who have already achieved success.

In looking into the lives of most self-made millionaires, the path that they followed was paved by them alone and the networks that they built. Rarely did it include their families and friends unless they were on the same mission. The ruthless spirit starts with breaking away from all those who you know were negative influences and having the faith, courage, and confidence to stand on your own—hence the term *self-made*. You did it yourself. It is not that you did not have help, but you broke all the bonds that were negative, and you refused to hold on to self-defeating thoughts or people who were stuck in their way of life.

In a nutshell, a consistent pattern of positive thinking, envisioning yourself being successful in any field that you choose, and allowing nothing or no one to deter you from that path is the seed of success. If you stay on this course, perfecting your craft along the way, paying homage, and learning the valuable lessons taught by others before you, then step by step, piece by piece, and day by day, you will deliberately and painstakingly build yourself into the successful person you see yourself becoming.

Conversely, to continue to dwell on thoughts (sometimes unconsciously) about failure or some other form of inability produces two things: a self-defeating attitude causing you to perform at levels far below what you're truly capable of, and a self-fulfilling prophecy. To think that you cannot do something causes you to not be able to do it. Convince yourself that you can do anything that you put your mind to. Refuse to accept failure, and you will not see it. When things do not go as planned, do not look at this as being indicative of you failing. Learn the lessons that are inherently found in things not going as you planned. Regroup and go back at it armed with more ammunition to propel you to success.

Look at your goals and set up a method or system that you will use to get you there. Use all the information, both positive and negative, as fuel. See no obstacle getting in the way of your success. Perhaps look at it like Napoleon Bonaparte did with his army. Upon invading one foreign land, he ordered his troops to burn all of the ships. He informed his troops that they would either "win or perish." They fought valiantly, knowing that they had no option of retreat. They won. According to some writers, Napoleon was one of the greatest military minds of his time, and he conquered untold lands.

"Win or perish." Win! Win! Win! Make up your mind to overcome all negative circumstances and always win regardless of what happens. Learn from every experience and keep a positive mind, and you will ultimately win.

CHAPTER 8

Love

There is a power in this world that has helped shape environments, people, and events. Every person is driven by this power, this force. It has two sides, one being extremely positive, which is love, and the other being extremely negative, which is hate. Unfortunately for the latter, it has a power that is very present in the world, and the end result is usually destructive. We shall not devote any energy to the matter of hate other than to acknowledge its existence say state that we should put all available means toward stomping it out. Both love and hate are very personal subjects, and as such this chapter will be a bit personal. As stated earlier, money should never be your primary objective. Money is a tool that is to be used to accomplish an objective, but it should not be the objective.

As an established or aspiring entrepreneur, you should be motivated by a drive that is nestled deep within your heart to provide some form of service to humanity. At the root of this drive should be a passion to help others live more comfortable lives, benefiting from the service that you can provide. The underlying motivating factor should be love—a love for God, yourself, your family, and your fellow man. This love does not have to necessarily be verbally expressed, but it should be shown in your commitment to your customers and your family. For your customers and clients, they can expect to always be treated with respect, courtesy, and professionalism. A high regard for standards and the motto of America's "E Pluribus Unum" (Out of the Many, One) should always be in your mind. Out of the many people, one nation, one aim, one goal, and one purpose: to provide service to its citizens that will make life more livable and more enjoyable. Let us refer to spiritual guru Deepak Chopra, who writes in *The Seven Spiritual Laws of Success*, "When you actions are motivated by love, your energy multiplies and accumulates - and the surplus energy you gather and enjoy can be channeled to create anything that you want, including unlimited wealth."[1]

Love is something that is inherent to us, and we feel its effect the moment we come to birth. Although we're not aware of it, we were surrounded by love, from the doctors who brought us here to our parents who nurtured us. Love has been present in and around most of us all of our lives. As we grow older, we learn to express it with those closest to us. We learn communication skills because of our love for those with whom we want to communicate. If we were to trace our growth from early on, it is primarily rooted in love. People love babies because they're so innocent and give love freely. Only when we are exposed to the harshness of life are we snapped out of our bubble and another reality starts to set in.

If not handled properly, our view of people can become negative, based on the influences around us. Love is not only an emotion that moves us and connects us to other people. It is also a principle that contains components that lead to success. Although this study details various principles designed to highlight the minds of successful people and the steps necessary to achieve success, love is so much deeper than mere success in the business world. Business, in fact, is the least important component of love, and money has very little to do with it. However, the principle of love is found in the very science of business. Commerce is large-scale business interaction, yet it is also the life blood of a community and nations.

In commerce, there are rules that allow for fair exchange of goods and regulations for up-to-date, wholesome products to be brought to market. This system of commerce is set up in America to provide quality products to the consumer, as well as afford an opportunity for entrepreneurs to create products and bring them to the public, as a form of servicing them with things that they can use to make their lives more pleasurable. At the root of this concept is the principle of love on a large scale.

On a smaller scale, you as the entrepreneur must also possess an appreciation for this process of commerce and fair exchange, and you must present yourself to this thriving market equipped with the right heart and mind. The educational system of business does not include the emotional side, but one does indeed exist. This does not mean that we enter business emotionally, but we must understand that at the root of every human interaction, there is an emotion.

We are connected to each other as people on an unconscious level. By providing a service and the customer paying for it, and by both parties showing their appreciation to each other, there is a connection and a subtle expression of love. We are loving creatures who can also become very destructive. This too cannot be erased from our nature.

It is of common opinion that if you are wealthy, this wealth provides you with a degree of power. Every person who has the ability to exercise power over others should have a genuine care and concern for the well-being of other people. This does not mean that you give all of your money away (see chapter 9), but there should always be a willingness to help others in some way. The person who has attained wealth and hoards it is not using money for its intended purpose.

With that being said, let us look at another stepping stone to building wealth with respect to love. A loving family is the cornerstone of the community, which is the foundation of a nation. How you build your home will help determine how you view the world and how you relate to it. Love at home builds a solid, peaceful person in the world, whether at home, at work, or elsewhere. A chaotic home cannot produce a productive, calm person. A stable home leads to a stable mind. A stable mind is a focused mind. A focused mind is a creative mind. A creative mind leads to a successful life. So much can be said about a stable home and how it shapes thoughts, attitudes, and behaviors.

A stable home starts with an organized union between husband and wife. If there is trouble in the home, as there inevitably will be at times, time should be dedicated to solving the problems with the heads of the household. It is said that in close quarters, emotions run deep. The key at times of trouble is a willingness by both parties to listen to the other person's complaints without becoming defensive. Again, the key is to listen. You cannot listen if you're talking. Let the other person speak his or her peace without being interrupted. At the end of the day, you all share many of the same things, including values, so it can be worked out if you listen and learn to communicate without being judgmental. This can be hard depending on the issue, but rest in the comfort that you love this person and want the best for him or her, so you sometimes compromise. Everything does not have to always go your way. Know that a united family is the building block of a successful business, community, and life. Work it out with love at the root. You do not have to always be right.

Family time is essential, especially at the dinner table. Here is where family plans are formed. Vacations, future events, and more are usually discussed over dinner. How wonderful it is for a family to enjoy a delicious meal together while planning future events that are designed to advance the family and plan fun adventures. Here is also where school, work, and other issues can be discussed. The goal is to unite your family's minds, causing them to think on one accord—the advancement of the family. Encourage your children to aspire for great things. Be a good example for them to live up to. Here is where your most important responsibilities reside. Always make time for your family; they are truly your backbone, so never make work more important than your spouse or children. Your first open-door policy should be at home. Make sure your children are comfortable in your office. Put them to work if your load is heavy. Think of ways they can help. Most of the time, they will be glad to do so because they get to spend time with you, and at the same time you're training them about the importance of business, deadlines, and more.

Learn to love life, enjoy your family, and always put them first. Loving your family and making them part of your business brings up to another component in the principles of love: loving your work. Loving what you do means that you may have indeed found part of your life's work. You're good at it, and it brings you a great deal of peace and calm. Congratulations to those who have found their life's work. Much can be said about you finding your purpose in life. Simply know that this indicates that all systems have lined up. "Blessed is the man or woman who finds their purpose in life."[4]

Having work that you truly enjoy doing and that also provides a service to others is indeed a good thing that can truly lead to happiness in other areas of your life. One of the first steps to gaining a truly fulfilling life is enjoying your work. Another is having a loving supportive family. With these two as part of your foundation, you are on your way. What is needed now is a systematic method of ascension. You have found the two most important components to building both a successful life and wealth. At the start of this ascent must be a clear resolve to maintain and increase your style of living. Your focus is mainly on the future. Love is at the root of your planning.

Preparation is now focused on building a good life for your family, and you want to make sure that your children have the ability to have all of the things that you were not able to enjoy while growing up. Care should be used to ensure that you do not instill the fears and worries that may have been with you during your upbringing. Time should have taught you to appreciate the finer things in life and the process it took you to get there.

The values you used to get you where you are should be the things that you pass on to your children. Again, let us bask in the beautiful light of wisdom shared by one of our great writers. Deepak Chopra shares some wisdom passed down through the ages in his book *The Seven Laws of Spiritual Success.* "We have stopped for a moment to encounter each other, to meet, to love, to share. This is a precious moment, but it is transient. It is a little parenthesis in eternity. If we share with caring lightheartedness, and love, we will create abundance and joy for each other. And then this moment will have been worthwhile."[2] Love is a force that not only shapes our present but also gives us hope for the future and a drive to create one for ourselves and those we love. From the richest to the poorest, we want the best for our children. Warren Buffett set up three dummy corporations worth $10 million apiece for his three children and gave one to each of them. He also said, "I told them I expected them to fail on some things, if they didn't fail they weren't doing important things."[3] The goals here is not only for Mr. Buffett's children to benefit from his wealth but also for them to use it for various charitable ventures, where the spirit of active service was being passed on to his children. Expecting them to fail should teach valuable lessons that would be useful later to perfect the acts of service.

In order to be successful, we must love our work. To build a successful home, we must love our family. Where there is love, there is life. However, this love is active. It is not merely the mushy, sentimental feelings. It is actions taken constantly, and it gives life to your ideas for the benefit of your family and business. It is love that gets us out of the bed in the morning and pushes us to overcome tremendous adversity and never give up. In essence, love is the root of life; without it, we will not thrive. Find what it is you love to do and what you're good at. Here is where you will flourish. If you do not presently love what you do, then keep pushing. Do not settle for anything less. You will never give your all to something that you do not love. If you do not give your all, you will never see the best you have, and you will not grow to new heights. In order to be at your best, you must find the thing that makes you want to do your best. Here, you will content your heart and discover your gifts. Dig deeper and hear your calling. Follow the voice. Go for the prize that you cherish in your heart. Seek to overcome every obstacle in your way and meet all challenges head-on. Your passions can become reality if you go after your dreams fearlessly. Love will be the force that is moving you. Do not resist it, because in so doing you get in your own way.

The surest way to realize your own potential is to act on your passions without fear or doubt. Do not be afraid to fail. If it is something that you're born to do, you will not fail. You will only get better with time. Build the life you want, starting with the things that you love the most. At every step, watch carefully because the future you envisioned becomes your present reality. Follow your heart; it is leading you to your destiny.

CHAPTER 9

The Money Principle

The properties of money are an issue misunderstood by many, because its possession is fleeting to them and long-standing to those who understand its true purpose. To some, money is an expression, a reflection of sorts of the energy used toward accomplishing a particular means. For others, it is of tremendous value simply because it allows them to buy what they want. The principles of money are not found in its expenditures but in its acquisition

Spending money is not only enjoyable but is a way of life. It is second nature to us without much consideration ever given to understanding the process of trade and commerce. The underlying principles, if understood, could not only teach us valuable lessons about money but may equip us to earn large sums of it. Let us start with some insight from one of the greats, Warren Buffett. "Money has given me the independence to do what I love daily. Beyond that it has no real utility for me but enormous utility for others, that's why I'm giving it away."[1]

In the past, money was anything that was generally accepted by people in exchange for the things they sell or the work they do. Today, it is mainly cash or credit. Today's society is largely based on credit. Cash has far less usage today than it did twenty-five years ago. With the broader range of credit, people find themselves in debt much easier than they were with the availability of cash. Today, you do not need cash if you apply for a credit card and receive it; you can buy now and pay later. This system has both benefits and harms. If you cannot afford to pay, you find yourself in debt. Roughly 50 percent of Americans have some form of credit card debt without a viable plan to pay it down. Although it should be made abundantly clear that debt is a part of life and should not be feared, how we acquire that debt, as well as what plans we have to pay on it, should be considered at the time the debt is acquired.

One of the first principle of money is its effective management. Here is a practice that can lead us up or down. It is also where spending habits are observed (discussed more in chapter 10). How you manage your money, first individually and then as a family, household, and ultimately a business, can lead to success or failure. There are many examples of companies going into bankruptcy because the people in charge of money did not handle it responsibly. The first official step to emotional stability and independence from Mom and Dad is learning how to manage our own money. And the first step is to being able to do so effectively is the need to take our emotions out of our spending habits. There is a psychological reaction to receiving money that we must get a grip on if we are to ever become efficient money managers. A mindset exists for those who have not developed the habit of keeping money, and that is to spend it. Those who have not yet grown used to always having money are constantly in a rush to get rid of it. I call it the "broke syndrome." It is a mental programming that many people readily accept where they must spend their money. As long as they have money in their pocket, their minds are consumed with ways to spend it. They will not rest until they have found ways to part with their money. The more they make, the more frivolous ways they come up with to spending it. They never develop the millionaire mindset. Regardless of how much money they make, they will still function with a broke mentality because they have not understood another key principle of money: saving.

So critical is the principle of saving to building a fortune that courses are taught on its importance. For the beginner, saving money instills several important qualities. Most important among them is discipline—the ability to abstain from spending money on things that you may want but not necessarily need at that time, even though you have the money to buy it. This helps with keeping your mind focused on the mission before you, delaying gratification until you have achieved a desired result. This discipline helps you put some of your lower urges in check before they get out of control. If these urges are not controlled and you begin to earn large sums of money, it could become your undoing. Thus, saving helps to give you control over yourself, and from this, control of your money. This is the primary reason for saving. From this, several other factors come into play dealing with how you think and how well you manage money, both yours and others.

Old Money vs. New Money

After saving your money and constantly earning more than you are spending, you start to grow comfortable with handling it. The longer this goes on, the more skills you acquire with the properties of money. Your mindset starts to change. You develop a somewhat aristocratic attitude. You have learned some important lessons about money and have managed to acquire a significant amount of it, and you now have an attitude toward money that is rather blasé. You do not look down on people, but money does not really impress you because you have had it for so long. Refer to the words of Warren Buffett at the beginning of this chapter. Buffett is a billionaire who has been wealthy for several decades, and he says that it has given him the independence to do what he wants to do, other than that it has no real utility for him, but it has tremendous utility for others, and that is why he is giving it away. This is the attitude of a billionaire. He has had money for so long and has accumulated so much that he is now helping others appreciate its properties. This is old money at play.

Generally, old money would be considered to be at least two to three generations past, creating a class of people literally born into money. It can also be first generation for those who have sustained wealth for over thirty years and have substantially increased it. For most, it comes by way of inheritance, passed on from generation to generation. Take for example the Fords. Henry Ford built an empire in his lifetime, amassing a large fortune. He groomed his son and grandchildren to continue the family business, and to this day, a member of the Ford family remains a majority shareholder in the family empire, the Ford Motor Company. The Ford position is no longer necessarily strictly about money. We will find present among the Ford family a dedication to the principles espoused by Henry Ford to provide service to humanity. There is a general attitude among this group that is rather elitist and removed from the masses. Most people with old money do not know what it's like to start a business from the ground up. Know that the end result of the daily struggle we endure now to prepare a better world for our children and grandchildren will one day put them in a class where they too will enjoy the benefits of old money. Meanwhile, rest assured that there is immense joy found in building this empire that your children and grandchildren will one day inherit.

New Money

Let us review the words of one of America's greatest presidents, Abraham Lincoln: "Property is the fruit of labor—property is desirable, is a positive good in the world. That some should be rich shows that others may become rich. And hence is just encouragement to industry and enterprise. Let not him who is houseless pull down the house of another, but let him work diligently and build one for himself, thus by example assuring that his own shall be safe from violence when built."[2]

New money can grow into old money in one's lifetime based on saving habits and the rapid accumulation of some revenue, if you start making money and continue to make money without interruption. While saving part of what you earn, your money begins to compound. You never spend the initial earnings made, creating old money over a long period of time and constantly earning more on top of what you already have. This tends to go on for many decades.

Many rags-to-riches stories would be in the new money category. There is an attitude present among many first-generation millionaires that is dynamic and deserves much attention, starting with the desire to give back. Let us refer to one of the greatest men of our era, Bill Gates: "Giving away money in meaningful ways will be a main preoccupation later in my life, assuming I still have a lot to give away."[3] Here again we find with another person who is very successful and who has the attitude of giving back. This has many elements to it leading, us to our next principle.

Money Circulation

The circulation of money is likened to the blood coursing through the body. Those who have accumulated large sums understand that their continued success depends on the constant circulation of money. Let us refer to some words of wisdom from Deepak Chopra: "Therefore, if we stop the circulation of money if our only intention is to hold on to our money and hoard it, since it is life energy, we will stop its circulation back into our lives as well. Like a river, money must keep flowing, otherwise it begins to stagnate, to clot, to suffocate and strangle its very own life force. Circulation keeps it alive and vita."[4] The circulation of money has both positive and negative effects. Several factors are considered in this process. The natural flow of money can take on patterns in our lives based on how we view it and what we do with it. I mentioned earlier that money should not be the primary goal in your pursuit of wealth. This may sound like a contradiction. Hence, we must first understand true wealth and the differences between having wealth and being rich.

Although a wealthy person is usually rich, you can be financially rich and not fully appreciate the value of true wealth. Having large sums of money in and of itself can qualify you to be rich. However, true wealth can be generational as well. Wealth is defined in economic terms as "value of assets—the value of assets owned by an individual or a community."[5] It is indeed a fine line, yet to gain an appreciation for riches, you learn to spend your money wisely, thus becoming wealthy. To spend money on frivolous ventures can be wasteful and will not yield any return other them temporary fulfillment. There is a place for this, but too much of it can lead to a diminution of money doing unproductive things, thereby wasting riches on things that do not hold real value. To purchase things of value such as investments, properties, gold, and oil, can and will lead to first an appreciation of money and then wealth.

Naturally, for the newcomers to the millionaires club, there will be time when money is wasted. However, time will reveal more purposeful uses for one's money. Thus, the circulation is not simply to give money away but to find creative uses for the dispensing of it. Family members who are not as fortunate as you will be a constant source of giving because they feel like part of your earnings is owed by virtue of them being related to you. That leads us to our next principle.

The People Tax

Family and friends who have not made the same decisions as you and may be in unfavorable conditions are, to some extent, entitled to your help and a small portion of your money. Consider it a part of you paying your dues, though it is not your responsibility to take care of the people outside of your household; by this I mean anyone other than immediate family. You do, however, have a responsibility to help people when you can, and only when to do so would not put any strain on your cost of living.

Call it a people tax that those who have become successful must pay as a means of gratitude. Although it may be the result of your hard work, dedication, and sacrifice that helped to put you where you are, if you look still deeper, you will find cooperation among some people who truly helped you achieve your success. Those less fortunate than you deserve some form of support, whether it is through some positive words of encouragement or financial assistance in some way. You owe a tax to the people. Try to keep a positive attitude toward those who are less fortunate and request help from you. Give it when you can. Be very careful, though, regarding how you do this. People can sometimes take your kindness for granted. The most important thing to do for those who seek your assistance is to give them sound advice about how to save money. When you find those who can truly use your help, and may even do the right thing with it, do all you reasonably can to help them.

Government Tax

Here is another way to look at it. The government taxes the people for several reasons. Nearly every person who earns a paycheck has to give a part of it to the government for the maintenance of the country. It may seem that a country that accumulates so much money should have not have to tax everyone. But once you reach retirement age, Social Security kicks in, and part of the money that you paid through the course of your lifetime now takes care of your monthly costs during your twilight years. It seems to be a burden to give some of your hard-earned money to the government, and they seem to tax everything. However, taxation is one of the guarantees of life. Regardless to your station, if you're being productive, you must pay your dues. There is no need to fight this system; do what you can to decrease your taxes, but in the end, it is unavoidable. Though this may seem like a negative, the government returns some of this money back to us, and those lump sums can become quite useful. This is the American way.

As said earlier, there is both a positive and negative side to money. The purpose of it on a positive level is to make life comfortable, happy, and luxurious. When you work hard, part of the reward is financial independence to be able to buy some of the things you want, to enjoy the freedom that money brings is wonderful. This freedom gives us the opportunity to not only enjoy life but to also look within ourselves and discover talents and abilities that can bring true peace. Money cannot buy happiness, so we cannot expend all of our talents simply on the acquisition of it. Those who do can enter into the negative side of money. It is another principle that we must also guard against.

Greed

Greed comes from an inordinate desire to acquire money, property, sex, food, or anything else to an excessive amount. It is classified as one of man's seven deadly sins and can lead to destruction. There is no place for greed in an open market. There is always room for the next person to grow. A desire to have it all, leaving no room for anyone else to prosper, will inevitably set one up for failure and disappointment.

Cash Flow

Now that some understanding has been reached about the various principles found in money, your goals have intensified to generate more of it. The flow of money into your hands will increase based on how well you have prepared to receive it. There is no discrimination as to where money will flow and to whom. What have you done and continue to do to receive it will determine the level of its flow into your hands. Being at the right place at the right time is also up to you. Things may not always come when you want them to, which means that more preparation is needed even though you may think that your time has come. Only when preparation and opportunity meet and you recognize and take advantage of it will your time come. Cash will always flow in and out of your hands. Depending on the type of work you do, the service you provide to others will play a large part in the amount that flows in. Your mindset toward money will determine whether it stays in your hands and continues to accumulate for you, or whether it travels right back out. It is all up to how you handle it.

Spendthrifts

We briefly touched on this, but now let us delve a little deeper into this mindset and how counterproductive it is to maintaining money and accumulating wealth. It is very difficult to be an accumulator of wealth and spend money wastefully at the same time. To be an extravagant spender, recklessly throwing money away on useless things, is unfortunately a reality for far too many people. Inside the households of some self-made millionaires, we will find a spouse who is a spendthrift. Arguments have ensued over the wasteful spending habits of the spouse who has found various reasons to buy things that usually remain on the shelf. Many of those types suffer from the broke syndrome and have embarked on a self-destructive path that will require some form of intervention. Spending money becomes as addictive as any drug, and the spendthrifts have become addicts. Shopaholies are the designation given to this type.

This addiction must be taken seriously, especially among those who plan to become millionaires and turn new money into old money. Credit cards may need to be canceled, probably giving rise to heated arguments. However, it is absolutely necessary to cease and desist wasteful, extravagant spending. Arguments are to be avoided as much as possible, but compromise and agreements start with a plan and a budget. Set aside a small amount for miscellaneous spending. Have the spouse agree to the budget, giving the spouse time and the freedom to gradually gain control of wasteful spending. Logically point out the frivolity of certain items purchased and encourage the use of coupons and other possible hobbies. Handle this matter gently and with intelligence and reason. If all else fails, resort to subterfuge and take all unnecessary credit cards. After the spouse calms down, sit down and have a heart-to-heart talk. Please be sure that your concerns are warranted and that you're not simply holding on to money too tightly. This leads us to our final negative principle.

The Miser

As stated earlier, money needs to circulate. It has no real use if we simply hold on to it, afraid to spend money because of our fear of being broke. It is important to have a healthy attitude toward money. If we have an unhealthy view of money, we will not afford ourselves the privilege of enjoying its properties. The primary purpose of money is that it be used to purchase the things we can afford. That will make our lives and the lives of our loved ones more enjoyable. We can never appreciate the full usage of money if we hoard it.

Let us look at it from a different angle. What we put out of life is what we get back. Once this life is over, we cannot take anything with us. If we make money and hold on to it tightly, what are the expected results? We work hard and do not use any of your hard-earned money to enjoy some of the pleasures of life. We then set up another set of circumstances. Say a man works hard, earns money, comes home, and relaxes. His money piles up in the bank, but time is going by. He is getting older and has missed out on many occasions to partake in the little pleasures because he does not want to spend any money. Time is still moving on, and he's getting older along with his family. He has built a comfortable nest egg, but he has passed on many of the little pleasures of life because he did not want to part with any money. He gets older and cannot do much anymore. His children now have moved on. He does take some pleasures with his grandchildren, but he has not fully enjoyed the beauty that having money can bring. He has a rather large bank account that will be divided up upon his death.

Although it is good to leave money for your family, you must take some of you hard-earned money and enjoy life. Let us reflect on some wise words from Mr. James Allen: "He who would accomplish little much sacrifice little; he who would achieve much must sacrifice much; he who would attain highly must sacrifice greatly."[6] We should be willing to sacrifice a place of what we earn to enjoy life. Life is too short to not take the time to enjoy the finer things that life has to offer. Being a miser takes some of the joy out of life. Work hard and play hard. Do not be wasteful, but enjoy life. Work to build a solid foundation for you and your family. Move out with a focused mind. Keep your goals in your mind and heart and enjoy your money.

CHAPTER 10

Lifestyle—Money, Power, Respect

The American lifestyle as a whole is one of indulgence and the gratification of desires. The American dream feeds the desire for success and comfort. The essence of the dream is responsible, but it can also lead to a life of excess. As an aspiring or established entrepreneur, you learn to take advantage of these desires and grow rich from them.

The United States exports a large share of its products for manufacturing purposes, but small businesses and large corporations are thriving within her borders. Trade and commerce are abundant, and opportunities are everywhere. Having a good understanding of the American lifestyle can be very helpful in your rise. Fundamentally, what drives America? Money. Second, what drives most people, American or otherwise? Love, money, and comfort. We have looked at some of the principles of money. Now, let us review how that money is earned and spent. America as a country is also driven by power and respect.

Money, Power, Respect

From the outside looking in, the United States is one of the most prosperous nations in the world, enjoying freedoms that many countries citizenry yearn for. To live in America as a citizen means that you get to enjoy many freedoms that others from afar can only admire and dream about. This freedom is normal to the average American, and so it is not fully appreciated and taken advantage of. For example, take American enterprise. The US government has established a system of trade and commerce that is completely free and open. Second, schools are set up to educate and train people for the business world. Many people have come to the United States with nothing but a desire to provide some form of service to others and build a family business. Structures are established to help direct these desires toward meaningful ends, providing financial assistance when suitable via the Small Business Administration and various financial institutions. Thus, you can simply come up with a viable plan inside the United States, and other people and businesses may choose to put their money behind you. In fact, regardless of how much money you may have as an individual, when you venture into the world of business, it would be wise for you to seek out investors such as banks and other lending institutions. The power of money in the United States of America lies in using it to make more money and to make money for others. Here lies the key in unlocking not only your potential but also the people with whom you associate.

It is a common opinion that birds of a feather flock together. Hence, you will find among your circle of friends a common bond that links each other to a similar goal. This is a very important process. Association breeds assimilation. Develop the right circle. Let's refer to one of the honorable ones, Mr. Bill Gates. "Maintaining focus is a key to success. You should understand your circle of competence, the things that you're good at, and spend your time and energy there."[1] This is not only how we can grow to perfection in our chosen field. We will also build a network of people with similar skills that will help us build up our business. The opportunities are all available. The lifestyle that you envision can be realized. The more understanding you have of the American way of life, the easier it will be to travel through the various stages. Those who do not make it to the top have many forces to which they can lay blame. However, if we look a bit further, we will likely find a breakdown somewhere in this pursuit. A total appreciation of the process is necessary, as well as an ability to function within the power dynamic of American business.

Power

In the business world, there are rules of engagement. Adherence to these rules can lead to advancement. Failure to observe them will usually lead to the destruction of your business. There is a link between business and politics. The higher we travel in the business environment, the clearer this becomes. Inside a democracy, money can help sway people. Most of this money comes from supporters of a particular candidate. There are reasons for this support. The money is used to help campaigns, get the message to more people, and gain more support. Search the background of most politicians, and you will find an intimate link with the business world.

From a business owner's standpoint, you must always be alert to changing tides that could affect the way your business functions, such as business tax, sales tax, and property tax. Once you have established yourself as a business owner, you want to maintain your position and grow stronger. At some point, local politics may become an issue for you. Once those in power notice that you're an established business, employing others and making contributions to the society, they may try and get you on a particular side, or your views may cause you to do so yourself. As a business owner, you have gained some degree of power.

You may wish to have a form of control or influence over your environment. Politics then becomes an issue for you. How you choose to use your money toward politics can bring about tremendous influence for you. People will respond to you favorably or unfavorably based on what you have done with your money.

If you have used it to help others, and if you have employed people and treated them fairly, then your money as well as your character will earn you the respect and love of your community, whereby you can potentially sway people to your views, creating another force. Many business owners and other professionals have found themselves entering into politics because they felt strongly about issues, have spoken to others in their respective communities, and quickly discovered that others not only share their views but also readily follow them and would support them for some political office.

For those who have not used their money wisely, have not gain considerable influence, and have not garnered the respect of the people, this is rare in business, because such types usually do not make it very far. These people were fortunate enough to inherit their parents' company but failed to learn from them how to deal effectively with people. They will either have to learn quickly how to handle others or hire someone who can. Suffice if to say that as your business grows, your power will also grow—power not only in politics but also in other areas of life.

Respect

As your status becomes more solid in the business environment and you become more proficient in handling matters of money, your power among the world gets stronger, and people start to see you in a different light. Respect is given to you in ways that you may not be used to. Be very careful here, because some have become quite puffed up due to how others treat them. Money breeds respect, and for those who do not have it or aspire to get it, they place those who have achieved it in high esteem for the most part. However, if the money is earned and no real character development has taken place, then you have not earned the respect that is given.

Learning how to earn large sums of money has attendant with it many responsibilities. Most important among them is how to treat people. It seems that people give you a great deal of honor and respect, but it starts simply as admiration because of what you have accomplished. During face-to-face time, the people get the opportunity to gauge your character and the level of respect you have for people. Fame is not necessarily a factor, except for those who have sought stardom. For these people, more attention is paid to their character and the manner in which they deal with people. If they're found to be disrespectful or contemptuous, they suffer the full wrath of the people. Why? Because it is the people who have lifted them up in acknowledgment of an exceptional talent. However, if it is found that their character is not receptive to the people, then people quickly turn on them, henceforth destroying them.

The entrepreneur suffers a similar disgrace in the business world. Everything depends on people, from those whom you employ to consumers. For the most part, business is people based. As such, a healthy respect for people is a must. Although it may seem for the successful that respect is always given to them, it must be returned in kind. A warning to those in business who do not have respect, honor, and appreciation for those who you're suppose to serve: Your success depends on how well you treat others, not how well they treat you. Part of this was discussed in chapter 8. Having a love for what you do will cause you to appreciate your work and the people you have working with you. Let us refer to the founder of Home Depot, Arthur Blank: "People can buy this merchandise somewhere else. The challenge is always remembering to walk in the customer's footsteps, not our own."[2]

For those who have become successful, respect is therefore something given to the people. Appreciation has to be shown. As a country, the United States of America is respected all over the world because of the freedom that it gives to its citizens. Whatever your abilities are will determine how far you rise in America. As a result, attention should be paid to the lower, middle, and upper class lifestyles and how they exist; why those in the lower class choose to stay in that condition; and those who have opted to take advantage of the many opportunities available. Let us start with a few words from Mr. James Allen: "In all human affairs there are efforts and there are results, and the strength of the effort is the measure of the result. Chance is not. 'Gifts,' powers, material, intellectual and spiritual possessions are the fruits of effort they are thoughts completed, objects accomplished, visions realized. The vision that you glorify in your mind, the ideal that you enthrone in your heart—this you will build your life by. This you will become."[3]

Herein, Mr. Allen has summarized the reasons why certain living conditions exist. Clearly it is based on thought and effort. Thereby, for those who dwell in America's ghettos, there is a specific reason why this environment continues to exist in a land of plenty. Let us take a trip to this environment, and we will find for the most part an attitude of self-defeat, where many drown their problems with drugs and alcohol. As a result, the condition persists. There is a solution to this problem that is just as certain as the problem itself, starting with a change of mindset. The perspective of most individuals who reside in the ghettos is one of escapism. Hence, a hard look is rarely taken at what continues to cause these harsh conditions. Blame cannot be placed on those who reside outside of these communities. The moment collective responsibility is taken, the environment will begin to change. Again, the opportunities are available. Those who change their views generally move on to suburban areas, or they live as such despite the conditions around them. We travel a bit further and reach the suburban lifestyle. Here too we find a mindset that is prevalent. For the most part, the suburban lifestyle is filled with people who are productive. The nine to fivers mainly reside here. They have an attitude of hard work and commitment. Typically these folks are workers. They help move the economy and are pretty comfortable. Here, we find the majority of Americans, and much can be learned about the American way. The realization of the American dream is found in many suburban homes.

Going to work, working hard, and respecting your fellow man. After a hard day's work, going to a comfortable home and a loving family, taking fun family vacations, and enjoying life. That is a large part of the American ideal. For those who do not aspire for great wealth and fortune, here is a happy medium. There are many millionaires who remain comfortably nestled in the middle also. Actually, many successful people remain here because the cost of living is not as expensive. It is cheaper than the rich neighborhoods where property tax and cost of living are higher.

Status Symbols

We cannot maintain our wealth if we constantly try to keep up with status symbols. Those millionaires who have chosen to maintain a middle-class way of life despite their ability to live in more affluent neighborhoods is indicative of their understanding of the money principle—that is a goal to save money. You can live very well and save money at the same time. Part of the reason why environments are as they are is largely due to the spending habits.

For example, for those who reside in more decrepit areas of the country, what is the degree of money circulation in that economy? Take for example Detroit, Michigan, a city that was taken over by a financial manager who declared bankruptcy for the entire city. Its leadership could not manage to pay its creditors. The politics of the city is a matter of discussion we will not have here, but let us look at the citizens. Detroit was also considered in 2013 "the most miserable city in America," and it ranked in the top five cities for murders. The crime rate is high, and unemployment ranks among the highest in the state of Michigan.

However, the general attitude of most of its citizens is one of surrender, producing a perpetual state of want. Travel throughout Detroit, and you will easily find liquor stores and large amounts of drug traffic. Although there is a significant amount of people employed, most of the business owners are not residents of Detroit. Thus, they take the money and run. Detroit citizens take the money they earn and spend it mainly outside of their communities, thereby causing no money to travel back through the city. Despite what the citizens spend their money on, there is no circulation. Businesses are thriving, but very little money is being put back into the city, causing a breakdown and leading to a need within the city to declare bankruptcy. There is a direct link to lack of control first over behavior, rooted in a disregard for the community. Youth are running out of control because of unconcerned parents who are too busy trying to gain control of their own lives. This lack of self-control causes lack of concern for the environment, creating dirty, deplorable streets and homes. Once there is no concern for the environment, there is no desire to invest in one's own home or community, so a large percentage are not homeowners. With a lack of concern for the environment, the money is spent on things that take them out of that environment. More specifically, no money is used to better the community. The end result is that crime and drugs are rampant. City officials dedicate more of the available resources on crime prevention, and little is actually spent on rebuilding the community. The end result is no real money circulation, despair, and a general attitude of misery. Hence the label "the most miserable city in America."

Bear in mind that most of Detroit's residents do not walk around feeling miserable. However, from the outside looking in, when statistics are studied, the conclusion is that these people are miserable. Being born and raised in Detroit myself, I cannot agree with the onlookers that we are the most miserable, but I can undoubtedly say that there is plenty of room for improvement, starting with the spending habits of its citizens and the lack of community based entrepreneurship. Unfortunately, the issues have deep roots, and it will take a complete change in leadership, as well as investments by both the people and the businesses. With hard work and time, Detroit will be true to the meaning of its seal, "Resurgent Ineribus," which means "It shall rise again from the ashes." Like many Detroiters, I am hopeful that the city will recover. Like her reverse side seal says, "Speramus Meliora," or "We hope for better things." We look to the horizon for better days.

Meanwhile, many people are fleeing the city life for the suburbs, saving their money, moving to better neighborhoods, and gaining a degree of comfort in the middle-class lifestyle. The spending habits for those who enjoy a more comfortable life are more credit based. A large percentage of these households have some amount of credit card debt. Consequently, this comfort comes at a price, which continues to create more debt. Most manage this relatively well, but others seem to get overwhelmed. The employment rate is higher, and there is more involvement with the community. The crime rate is lower, and the attitude is generally to be productive.

There is an attitude of comfort and happiness for those who reside in the middle. There is no plan by most people in the middle to own and operate their own businesses. They have jobs that pay the bills, and they're content with the way that things are. The goal may be to push their children to adventure further up the ladder by way of furthering their education, but many of the parents have found comfort and contentment with their middle-class life. In many ways, this will help the aspiring entrepreneur to achieve greater things. Those in the middle who have become comfortable with this life are mainly consumers. They go to work but are not responsible for producing most of the products that they use.

This should never be looked upon negatively. It is not the role of everyone to produce or sell the products that the average family uses. Although the opportunity is available to everyone, it is not taken advantage of. You should happily fill this void if you can find a product that the people want. This can be very helpful in your climb. It is not necessary that you create something new. The people's needs are quite simple and will not vary much from state to state and country to country. Let us refer to economist Gary Shilling: "Play in your own sandbox. Don't try to reinvent the wheel. Most of us will be better off in terms of what we can do for the world by just intelligently and efficiently applying what is already known."⁴

Here is some good advice for those who aspire to be of service in some way. To find your niche where you can best serve and benefit yourself and the community, study spending habits first. Here, you will find what the people like most and how they spend their money. You can understand the lifestyle of the people in any particular area. This suggests that we do not have to necessarily have any exceptional talent, but that we simply harness the ability to tune into people's wants and needs. As a general rule of thumb, people base their spending habits on four categories: food, clothing, shelter, and entertainment, and not necessarily in that order. To be of service, find something in any of these categories and go about establishing your brand. A great place to start is with the people who reside in the middle.

Travel a bit further, and we get to the rich. What are the spending habits of the rich? What do they usually buy? In dealing with the spending habits of the rich, we will surprisingly find that many millionaires are very savvy spenders, always looking for ways to save a buck. Ironically, many first-generation self-made millionaires are very mindful about what they buy on a daily basis. We will find that many of them are not busy trying to keep up with the latest fashion or purchase products based on trend. Their primary focus is on the luxuries at home. Thus, money is frequently spent on amenities for the home, comfort, efficient vehicles, and clothing. Professionals are often sought by the rich to provide some form of services. Nannies, housekeepers, drivers, and other services are usually provided. Shopping for clothes is usually done at high-end stores because of the nature of most successful people: they like order and organization. Consequently, professional services are usually preferred because of their efficiency.

There is, however, a class of millionaires that are extremely wasteful with their money. They usually fall from the millionaires' club after a number of years. Many entertainers waste millions doing frivolous things daily, such as making it rain in a club with cash, or spending two million dollars on a pair of diamond-laced shoes. This type of wasteful spending is frowned upon by most millionaires as being rather foolish and indicative of a person not having enough creative things to do with money. However, the jewelers and nightclub owners welcome this type. Hence, these millionaires do serve the purpose of helping money circulate. This is usually not conductive to maintaining wealth, however.

How the rich remain rich is a question, and the answer can lead to a life of continuous financial success and prosperity. There are many variables at play to keep the rich that way, starting with loopholes in taxable income. Finding ways to move the earned money around and allowing it to increase, is also a significant way to maintain wealth.

Portfolios

Having a portfolio of investments puts you on a path to money management. Finding good investment options and putting some of your earnings to the side for different possible investments puts your mind on the right track. Watching the stock market and real estate market, and keeping alert to the numerous options that come open at any given time, will be very helpful in using your money to make more. The key here is to understand that it takes money to make money. You must find ways to use your money to make more. Regardless of your business savvy, it is always good to seek the advice of professional financial planners to help develop a portfolio and direct you toward wise investment choices.

Fundamentally, those who have gained wealth tend to stick to the same path that brought them their wealth from the beginning. They learn well their craft and stay in that field. When they do venture off, they do so carefully. James Allen said, "Victories attained by right thought can only be maintained by watchfulness. Many give way when success is assured, and rapidly fall back into failure."[5]

There is also a pretty simple principle that must be observed by the rich to maintain their riches. They do not associate too closely with those who do not have money. Let us take to heart the wise words of Nelson Mandela: "Many people will appear to befriend you when you're wealthy, but precious few will do the same when you are poor."[6] Be very careful with whom you befriend once success arrives. Many will expect you to always foot the bill for them. There is a reason why some people have and others have not. This is largely due to the thinking patterns. If you constantly spend your money on people who have none, you will soon join them!

EPILOGUE

The road to becoming wealthy is a very deliberate, painstaking, and concentrated process. It does not happen overnight and is normally filled with many setbacks, roadblocks, disappointments, and failures. Those who look at successful people and admire their success rarely consider the pain, hard work, sacrifice, and dedication it took for these people to get where they are.

Talk to most self-made millionaires, or people in general who have gained success to some degree or another in their respective fields, and they will each have a story to tell. Many of those stories may bring up painful memories, because the road to success is filled with people who have felt that they have been let down, betrayed, or disappointed. Many of these people are the close family members and friends of the rich and successful. Success and wealth is to be celebrated and studied. However, hurt feelings, losses, disappointments, failures, many long days, and sleepless nights accompany those who have made it to the top.

To understand what it takes to be successful in the world of business is to be aware of both the good and the bad. As to everything in life, there is polarity. Positive and negative points. Good and bad sides. The sun does not shine every day; there will be rainy days. We will all suffer our share of losses and enjoy our days of victories and successes. We must learn to find the good in the bad and reap the benefits of it. We must learn from our wins so that we can keep winning, and we must appreciate it from a focused mind, where we do not stand in awe of our own accomplishments or the accomplishments of others.

There is a step-by-step process to achieving anything you want in life. Start first with a focused, determined mind. My father told me at the age of eight years old, out of frustration at his inability to help me with my homework, to not take *no* for an answer. At that time, I had no clue what he meant and what it had to do with my homework. Yet something told me that what he had just said to me was far more important than any lesson my teachers could teach me. Because of these words spoken to me by my father, I have become successful in life not because I have not failed at times but because I refuse to give up.

He taught me to never stop until I get what I want, regardless of the obstacles that I must overcome. This applies to you too. Never give up, and never give in. Fight through everything until you reach your goals. As a young boy, this teaching hurt me in some ways. But as I grew older, I began to understand that this mindset is present in a small but very powerful segment of the population. Those people are usually rich and successful. This success I found was rooted in the same principle that my father taught me as a young boy. These people refuse to give up. No matter what came into their lives, they would not quit. Something inside of them drove them forward, and they were willing to overcome all obstacles to meet their goals. These people would not take *no* for an answer. They saw something in their minds and refused to let it go. They refused to give up on their dreams. There is a mindset present in this group of people that is so dynamic, so radiating, and so transforming, and if we study this mindset and develop some of its traits, we will gravitate toward success. We will draw it to us because the spirit we embody quite simply is one of success.

What we have done here is look closely into the lives of a multitude of millionaires and billionaires and develop principles that, if followed, can lead to success and riches. It is not a quick fix formula; it is a mental process that will cause action and will lead to success. However, the right mental attitude is everything. If we do not have the right attitude, we will deny ourselves many of the things that are so readily available to us. Having a clear vision means in part that your views are not based on your emotions—that is, how you feel about a particular situation from moment to moment. Being an effective decision maker means that you decide with your head, not your heart.

Acceptance is key—this does not mean that you have to live with a certain situation, but once you see it for what it is, you accept that you may need to change it. The scope is broad from a visualizing standpoint. Accept in your mind the life you want. Then the work starts. How do you bring this vision into reality? Working on this vision can take years, and all the steps included in the previous chapters will help in that process. It is an enjoyable work, all the more so if you're doing something that you love to do. As stated earlier, there will be negatives, but you must not let these negatives deter you. If it is something that you love to do and believe that it is your calling, you will see nothing but success coming to you.

Finally, the American dream is not only something that most Americans aspire to. People in many countries throughout the world aspire for the things that the American dream defines. The good job, the beautiful home with the white picket fence, the nice cars, and the happy family are things that people all over the world strive for. Those in America call it one thing, and people in other countries may call it something else. Regardless of the names, the goal is to find happiness. It has often been said that money cannot buy happiness. Yet success itself brings about a sense of peace of mind through accomplishments and productivity. Here, we also find happiness.

Self-Made

Self-made is defined as being "successful as a result of work. Successful or wealthy through your own effort, rather than through birth or from the work of others."[1] This work is strictly about the self-made millionaires and billionaires and the fundamental rules that must be adhered to in some way. It is specific to becoming and remaining successful. Success in life as a whole is filled with rules. These rules are based on universal laws that are exact in human nature. Regardless of what your religious beliefs are, there is a cause and effect law that cannot be denied. If you continue to promote a certain cause, you will eventually get the effect that you strive for. If you strive for success, dedicating your time and energy to this goal, you learn what you need to learn, following the well-lit path toward this end. With patience and persistence, you will achieve your desires.

I have sought to give an outline to this journey, providing insight to the up-and-coming and inspiration to those who have already partaken in this journey. The road ahead is unforgiving. It is not a course to be entered haphazardly. For those who simply want wealth and are not willing to do the work and develop the mindset necessary to achieve it, stop now and reevaluate your thinking. This is not a road for the faint at heart or those who have not given serious consideration to this process. Do not get in the way of those who have their minds set on becoming successful and wealthy because you will become a casualty. Take the time to develop your thoughts, learn well the lessons, and go for it.

To the serious-minded individuals who have held deep in their hearts and seen clearly in their minds the image of themselves becoming successful and wealthy, the path has been set for us. The lessons have been taught; learn them well. The sacrifices have been made. The world awaits our coming. Keep these principles in mind and always respect the craft. Always hold the people in high regard and go get it. It is there waiting for you. Call it into existence; it will not hold itself back from you. Believe that you will be successful and wealthy, and you will be. Look neither to your right nor your left. Go get it, keeping your eyes, mind, heart, and soul on the future. You will win. Good luck.

Best wishes for your continued success.

Konato Williams

ENDNOTES

Chapter 1

1. Encarta World English Dictionary, s.v. "vision."
2. *World Book Encyclopedia* (2001), s.v. "Andrew Carnegie."
3. World Book Encyclopedia (2001), "Dale Carnegie."
4. *Entrepreneur Magazine*, March 2011, 104–105.
5. Quote from Leon Black, *Entrepreneur* 41, no. 11.
6. *World Book Encyclopedia* (2001), s.v. "Henry Ford."
7. *World Book Encyclopedia* (2001), s.v. "Kennedy Dynasty."
8. *World Book Encyclopedia* (2011), s.v. "Bill Gates."
9. John F. Kennedy, inauguration address, 1961.
10. Queen Latifah, Coke advertisement.
11. Dale Carnegie, *How to Win Friends and Influence People*.
12. *Black Enterprise* 41, no. 11 (2010).
13. *Black Enterprise* 41, no. 11 (2020).

Chapter 2

1. Encarta World English Dictionary, s.v. "leadership."
2. Interview with Bernard Beal, CEO, M. R. Beal and Co., *Black Enterprise,* August 2010.
3. Bill Gates, *The Road Ahead*, 208.
4. Quote from Henry Ford found in *How to Win Friends and Influence People*.
5. On Burrell Communications Group LLC, *Black Enterprise* (August 2010).

6. Bill Gates, "Leaders Must Be Candid, Consistent," *New York Times,* September 12, 1996.
7. Burrell Communications Group and Fay Ferguson, *Black Enterprise,* August 2010.
8. Old Chinese proverb, Sage of the Ages.
9. Jeff Clavier, *Entrepreneur Magazine,* 2011.
10. McGhee Williams Osse, *Black Enterprise,* August 201.
11. Sheryl Sandberg, *Forbes* 193, no. 4.

Chapter 3

1. Research on motivation found in World Book Encyclopedia (2001).
2. *World Book Encyclopedia* (2001), s.v. "Rothschilds."
3. World Book Encyclopedia 2001, s.v. "personality."
4. T. Boone Pickens interview, *Forbes Magazine,* Spring 2014.
5. *Encarta World Dictionary*, s.v. "motivate," "motivated," and "motivation."
6. Interview with Drew Brees, *Entrepreneur Magazine* 38, no. 8 (2010).
7. Dylan Smith, *Entrepreneur Magazine,* August 2010, 78.
8. Eddie C. Brown, *Black Enterprise* 41, no. 11.
9. Michael Steinhardt interview, *Forbes* 193, no. 2: 70.

Chapter 4

1. Encarta World English Dictionary, 512.
2. Mark Cuban interview.
3. Bill Gates, "Ask Bill," *New York Times,* 1995.
4. Thomas T. Stanley and Williams D. Danke, *The Millionaire Next Door: The Surprising Secrets of America's Wealthy.*
5. *Forbes* 192, no. 5: 122.
6. *Encarta World English Dictionary*, s.v. "preparatory measure."
7. The Roberts Bros. Properties, *Black Enterprise* 41, no. 11.

Chapter 5

1. Interview with Drew Brees, Entrepreneur Magazine 38, no. 8 (August 2010).
2. *World Book Encyclopedia* (2001), s.v. "Study on John Davison Rockefeller."
3. United States Declaration of Independence.

4. Bruce Greenwald, *Entrepreneur Magazine*, 2010.
5. John Chambers, *Forbes* 193, no. 6.
6. Drew Brees interview, *Entrepreneur Magazine,* August 2010.

Chapter 6

1. Encarta World English Dictionary, s.v. "cooperation."
2. *World Book Encyclopedia* (2001), "cooperatives."
3. Bill Gates, "What Makes a Good Manager," *New York Times,* Special Feature, 1997.
4. Dave Duffield, *Forbes* 193, no. 5.
5. The Roberts Brothers, *Black Enterprise* 41, no. 11.
6. Barbara Corcoran interview, *Entrepreneur Magazine*, March 2012, 60.
7. Corcoran interview, *Entrepreneur Magazine*, 60.
8. Karen G. Mills, *Entrepreneur Magazine*, August 2010.
9. Napoleon Hill, *Law of Success.*

Chapter 7

1. Roget's II: The New Thesaurus, 3rd ed., s.v. "doubt."
2. *Roget's II: The New Thesaurus,* 3rd ed., s.v. "faith."
3. James Allen, *As a Man Thinketh (Thought and Purpose).*
4. *World Book Encyclopedia*, s.v. "History of Abraham Lincoln, Famous Pleas, 1860 Cooper Union Ney Work."

Chapter 8

1. Deepak Chopra, The Seven Spiritual Laws of Success, 55.
2. Chopra, 111.
3. *Forbes 400 Billionaires*, October 2013.

Chapter 9

1. Quote from Warren Buffett.
2. Abraham Lincoln, Reply to Workingman's Association, March 21, 1864, in *World Book Encyclopedia* (2001).
3. Bill Gates, "Ask Bill," *New York Times*, August 1, 1995.
4. Deepak Chopra, *Seven Spiritual Laws of Success*, 29.
5. *Encarta World English Dictionary.*

6. James Allen, *As a Man Thinketh*.

Chapter 10

1. Bill Gates, New York Times, 1997.
2. Arthur Blank, *Forbes* 192, no. 5.
3. Allen, *As a Man Thinketh*.
4. Quote from Gary Shilling.
5. Allen, *As a Man Thinketh*.
6. Nelson Mandela, *Long Walk to Freedom*, 78.

Epilogue

1. *Encarta World English Dictionary*, s.v. "self-made."